Percy

The perspicacious memoirs of a cricketing man

To Mike
Best Wishes

Percy

The perspicacious memoirs of a cricketing man

Pat Pocock
with
Patrick Collins

Foreword by Micky Stewart

© PAT POCOCK 1987

Published in Great Britain by
Clifford Frost Publications

Book design by Peter Frost
Reproduction by Sinclair Graphics
Typeset, printed and produced by
Clifford Frost Ltd
Lyon Road   Wimbledon SW19 2SE

ISBN 1-870066-02-2

All rights reserved

Acknowledgements

To Patrick Collins,
who inspired me to recollect,
then sifted, sorted, collated
and arranged my memories,
I offer my sincerest thanks —
his professionalism and sense of humour
made my task a real pleasure.
I would also like to thank
a dear friend, Peter Frost,
who suggested the book
and helped to bring it to fruition,
and Patrick Eagar and Adrian Murrell
for their great help with photographs.
To my family,
who have shared the joys and frustrations
of my cricket career,
and to those who appear in this book,
I owe a great debt —
without you I would have missed out
on a lot of fun,
and had so much less to chat about.

Dedication

To the players who have given me
enough enjoyment for a lifetime
in the space of 23 years,
especially
Micky Stewart
Robin Jackman
Intikhab
and Gary Sobers.
I am only sorry it had to end.

Contents

	Page
Foreword	11
Chapter One Percy Pocock! That's your name from now on, lad	13
Chapter Two He's another one stringing you a line	18
Chapter Three I'll let you have a bouncer in the morning	23
Chapter Four He was the kindest, most gentle character in cricket	31
Chapter Five If I tell him all my secrets, he'll finish up pinching my place	36
Chapter Six We'll keep a welcome in the hillside	46
Chapter Seven I've already worked him out. But don't go telling the others	54
Chapter Eight Come on Basil. If you get out now we can beat these white men	58
Chapter Nine Oh, well, perhaps I did get a touch	63
Chapter Ten Will somebody tell me what is happening	70
Chapter Eleven Do me a favour, Perce. Bring me back a Mars bar	78
Chapter Twelve Come on, Greigy, I think you'd better let me drive you home	87
Chapter Thirteen Don't even try to get him out	97
Chapter Fourteen A bunch of chimps were worth six times as much as a Test cricketer	103
Chapter Fifteen Our fellows got carried away	107
Chapter Sixteen I see you're only booked in for two nights	115
Chapter Seventeen Don't go on too long about the cricket	122
Chapter Eighteen Getting blown away on a cricket field is a bit different	133
Chapter Nineteen We scooped up more oranges and resumed our attack	140
Chapter Twenty Strange how old black and white pictures slow down the action	153
Chapter Twenty-One Be very certain about it, Perce. You're a long time not playing	160
Career Statistics	165
Illustrations	166
Index	167

Foreword

When Pat Pocock decided that the day had come for him to retire from first-class cricket after a career spanning twenty-three years, the game not only lost an outstanding player, but also one of its greatest fans. Throughout his time in the game, Pat maintained his original schoolboy enthusiasm for his profession and was a credit to cricket both on and off the field.

It was my pleasure to be the captain of Surrey when Pat made his debut, and to take an early catch off his bowling, to set him on the road to his first-class cricket haul. He approached this match with supreme confidence, and was never reluctant to state exactly what he wanted when discussing the placing of his field. He was forever studying batsmen's techniques, looking for every little weakness which he might take advantage of when bowling to them. This meticulous attitude was part of his nature, and you knew the kind of man you were dealing with when you looked into his cricket case and saw that every article of equipment was neatly packed and bore his trademark of 'PO'.

Pat Pocock will forever be remembered as 'Percy', his nickname in cricket from very early days. It was given to him by the then Surrey physio, Sandy Tait, a real character and humorist. A 'proper Percy' was what Sandy called him, and it suited him down to the ground, particularly when he went out to bat, with his bouncing walk and his air of gloriously unfounded optimism.

Where Percy was, there was always a smile, and I am sure there always will be. Pat Pocock was a fine bowler and a very fine ambassador for the game of cricket, and I am very pleased to have played so many past seasons with him.

MICKY STEWART *April 1987*

Chapter one

Percy Pocock!
That's your name from now on, lad

PERCY was born on a warm August evening in 1964. He was the brainchild of one Sandy Tait, an elderly tyrant with a taste for juvenile humour. Over the years, Percy would occasionally curse his creator and wish that his wit had run to something more dignified. But the feeling never lasted long, for it was a comfortable name and people smiled when they spoke it. All things considered, the old tyrant had chosen well.

In fairness, I have to say that Tait never intended such a happy outcome. He had spent half of his seventy years rubbing the limbs and bending the ears of generations of Surrey players, and his experience had taught him that young cricketers were to be neither tolerated nor trusted. They mocked his homburg hat and his stiff leg and his habit of addressing the county Secretary as 'Sir'. They ruined his ancient jokes by blurting out the punch-lines, and on away trips with the county side, the bolder ones would steal his razor and hide his clothes. It was the kind of treatment which might have defeated a lesser man, but as the resident Surrey 'character', Tait simply dedicated himself to the task of putting the upstarts in their place.

Like so many of his generation, he believed that privilege was the prize of seniority and he enforced his code without mercy. I remember travelling up for a game at Northampton and checking into a residential pub. It was a noisy establishment on the side of a busy hill, and its windows would rattle as the heavy lorries worked through their gears. By chance, I was the first Surrey player to arrive and in my youthful brashness I asked for a quiet room at the back.

I was half-way through the request when Tait crashed through the front door. 'Quiet room at the back!', he roared.' Hell fire! Who d'you

CHAPTER ONE

think you are? You'll wait for the captain and the senior pro and everyone else in this team who's seen a bit of service, my lad. Then we'll see what kind of room you get.'

He was just the same when cricket bats were sent in to be autographed. Occasionally, I would scribble a preoccupied signature half-way up the blade. Tait would explode. 'Since when does the junior pro sign bats half-way up?', he would shout. 'You sign at the bottom because that's your place. And remember you're lucky to be on the bat at all.'

As the Surrey masseur, Tait recognised and respected the fact that many people outranked him in the Oval pecking order. He would never enter a dining room alone, preferring to lurk in the foyer until a senior player drifted through. And if a committee member should put his head in the dressing room, Tait would fall over himself to brew tea and hunt down biscuits. But he retained a licence to persecute those whom he considered inferior. He bullied dressing room attendants with such venom that they never lasted more than a month, and junior pros were God's gift to his ponderous wit.

I never had a chance, for a man who had soothed the aching muscles of Laker and Lock was unlikely to hold a seventeen-year-old spinner in excessive respect. In my early days at Surrey, I lost count of the times when I would return from a hard day in the field to find that my jacket pockets and trousers had been sewn up. 'Taity's been in', the older players would say.

Deep down, I suspect that Tait realised that he was one of the last of his breed. The days of Gentlemen and Players had departed, much to his disapproval. Social distinctions were less rigid and the county cricket dressing room was one of the few remaining hideaways where a man of seventy could play the spoons, belt out old music hall songs, tell the old stories and win the friendship of young men with adolescent practical pranks. He set great store by those pranks, and it was not until I fell victim to his favourite ploy that he regarded me as a bona fide member of the Surrey team.

I was watching a match from the players' balcony one day when Tait approached and stood next to me. He produced a small bottle half full with alcohol in which floated a dead fly, a small cork and a tiny piece of grit. For a couple of minutes, he stood there shaking the bottle in front of his face. 'What are you up to, Taity?', I said, but he didn't answer. After a few more moments, he passed me the bottle. 'You have a go', he said, so I gave the bottle a long, serious shake, and I was only vaguely aware that I was surrounded by senior players; Ken Barrington, Micky Stewart, John Edrich and the rest. At last, my patience snapped. 'What the hell am I trying to do, Taity?', I said. He replied: 'You're trying to get that bubble up that fly's bum'.

*Sandy Tait,
creator of 'Percy'
and the life and soul
of the Surrey dressing room
down the decades*

CHAPTER ONE

The whole team fell about. 'Taity's done another one', they yelled, and there was much hand-shaking and back-slapping and for the rest of that day, old Sandy Tait looked the happiest man in the world. 'I really enjoyed that, but the best day was when I was masseur to the England team, and I caught Len Hutton with the Fly in the Bottle, right in the middle of a Test match. That was the highlight of my career.'

Tait was in the dressing room on that August day when I played my first championship match for Surrey in the traditional Bank Holiday game against Nottinghamshire. He saw me brought on to bowl an hour before lunch, saw the captain, Stewart, set my field, he saw Ian Moore caught at slip by Stewart Storey off my fifth ball in championship cricket and he saw me bowl twenty-two consecutive overs for figures of 3 for 68. Then he watched me collapse with cramp in the middle of the Oval, and that pleased him most of all.

He was efficiency itself when they delivered me back to the pavilion, dumping me in a hot bath and debating various courses of treatment. But he was spared a decision by the appearance of Bill Tucker, a London orthopaedic surgeon. Tait stood to attention and rapped out the details: 'Sir, this young chap. Bowled a long spell. Hot day. Gone down with cramp. What do you suggest, Sir?' Mr Tucker prescribed salt tablets, and a manic grin split Tait's face. He reached for a dusty jar and produced two tablets the size of small golf balls, which he gleefully forced down my throat as I gagged and choked.

Half an hour later, I shuffled back to the field where Ron Tindall, our middle order batsman, asked for details of my cure. 'Salt tablets,' I said, 'Taity says he swears by them.' Tindall rushed off to tell the others, and as I looked around the ground, I could see ten Surrey cricketers staring and pointing and laughing at me. Ken Barrington let me into the secret just before close of play. 'That Taity came to the Oval thirty-five years ago', he said, 'and on the day he arrived, he brought that jar of salt tablets with him. He's been searching for somebody mug enough to take them ever since'.

I went searching for Tait with all the indignation that a seventeen-year-old victim could command. I found him in the dressing room, surrounded by players and enjoying his hour of triumph. 'You knew they were thirty-five years old', I yelled. And he smiled that terrible smile. 'True enough,' he said, as he rolled his perpetual dog-end from one side of his mouth to the other, 'but they did the trick. Admit it, young Percy Pocock, they did the trick all right'.

The players were on to it in a flash. 'Percy Pocock! That's perfect. Dead right. Taity, you're a genius'. The smile never left the old devil's face as he shrugged and bowed and accepted a drink. Sandy Tait was in his rightful position, on centre stage in a Surrey dressing room, leading the lads in a joke and scoring off one of those cheeky kids at the same time. It wasn't the same as catching out Hutton with the Fly in the Bottle, but it would carry him nicely through a three-day game with Notts.

He was still chuckling when I left for home. 'Percy!', he said, 'Percy Pocock! That's your name from now on, lad. You're stuck with it'. And, for once in his life, he was right.

Chapter two

He's another one stringing you a line

THE summer of 1956 witnessed two significant yet entirely unconnected sporting landmarks. Jim Laker took nineteen Australian wickets for ninety runs at Old Trafford, and I became the official scorer to Merton Cricket Club. Laker, for his efforts, received the acclaim of a grateful nation; I received the satisfying sum of half a crown per match. As one who was growing to love the game, I was aware of Laker as the distant god, the man who was held up as the ultimate example to any Surrey youngster who attempted to bowl off-spin. With the innocent arrogance of youth, I believed that if I worked hard enough, I could bowl pretty acceptable off-spin. Just like Jim Laker.

I was fortunate in my tutors. A drama teacher named Barry Willett, a wonderful eccentric who wore pyjamas beneath his suit, taught me how to grip the ball, and I worked for ungrudging hours in the nets to acquire the rudiments of line and length. By the age of twelve, I was playing for Merton's first team, a substantial club side with a smattering of ex-pros who were vastly amused to find a child prodigy in their ranks. They were captained by John Keeping, a constant source of encouragement. Kind men, they not only steered me away from the most basic mistakes and allowed me to buy my wickets at considerable cost, they also parked me outside the pub door after matches and kept their juvenile off-spinner supplied with lemonade and crisps. My parents were similarly supportive and possibly a little mad. I passed the thirteen-plus exam which enabled me to move from Merton Church of England Secondary Modern School to Wimbledon Technical College, but the headmaster of the Tech was unwilling to indulge my cricketing fantasies. For an embryo Laker who was by now intent on making his way in professional cricket, the situation was intolerable, and I demanded a transfer. My parents, revealing a tolerance which appeared remarkable only in my later life, gave their assent, and I left the faintly prestigious college to return to the Sec Mod, with its proper appreciation for God's own game. I repaid my debts to parents and school by going on to play for England Schools, for whom I made fifty-three absurdly elegant runs. At that stage, I was a bowler with strong and subsequently unfulfilled ambitions to become an all-rounder. But my general form in club and schools cricket had attracted the notice of important people. Rumour suggested that a gentleman from the Oval would soon be in touch with me. And rumour, thankfully, was absolutely correct.

The phone call came from Arthur McIntyre, the former England wicket-keeper, Surrey coach and a man deeply immersed in the tradition of the county. He showed me all the important features of the ground; the upstairs room where the amateurs had changed in bygone days and the nail upon which he had hung his clothes when the club had carried a staff of thirty-five. He also promised to pay me £5 a week for a year's trial, and I thanked him more times than was decent. I was sixteen years old and I had arrived. I travelled from Merton each day by bus and tube and I never tried to hide the fact that the Oval was my destination. Being a gregarious chap, I quickly adopted a familiar tone with the senior pros. I called Barrington 'Kenny', Bernard Constable became 'Bernie', and I drew the line only with Micky Stewart, who was always 'Skipper'. I worked hard in the nets and at fielding practice, and I was far too young to recognise the physical training for the farce that it was; a little running, a touch of sprinting and a few exercises. Fifteen minutes, no more. Fitness was a concept which professional cricketers refused to embrace.

After a few months I made the second team and my wages soared to £15 a week. My friends at the youth club in South Wimbledon regarded me as something of a tycoon. But if the money was welcome, then the opportunity to learn the game from accomplished players was invaluable. The seniors all helped in their various ways, but I had virtually no contact with the man who had most to impart. Tony Lock was then in his last season at Surrey and I had heard a few unpleasant things about him. He was said to be a moody, occasionally fiery man, an aggressive loner who enjoyed his own company and resented intruders.

One evening, during that first year, I took a box of balls to a bowling net at the Oval. Now that really is a hard, frustrating exercise; bowling six balls at a wicket in an empty net, then walking

CHAPTER TWO

down to pick them up and trudging back to repeat the practice over and over again. But I had to do it because I needed to learn to pivot a little more in my delivery stride. I'd been at it for about twenty minutes when I saw a figure coming out of the dressing room and walking across to meet me at the Vauxhall End. "What are you working at?", said Lock, and I explained. For the next hour he took me through my action; suggesting, hinting and demonstrating how I could get the best from my efforts. The whole staff had gone home, but the great man stayed because he had found a raw kid who wanted to learn. It was a marvellous gesture, and I never listened to any more dubious tales about Tony Lock after that session.

Several years passed before I felt able to consult Lock's famous counterpart, the man with whom I had helped make 1956 such a memorable season for English cricket. I had not wanted to presume on Jim Laker's good nature, while he had been reluctant to press his advice upon a young off-spinner who was trying to make his way. When I finally approached him, he offered thoughtful tips and considered comments, but his greatest contribution was the simple recognition that the game had changed beyond measure since his own playing days. He conceded as much after one particularly painful Surrey match against Gloucestershire which saw Mike Procter, the supremely accomplished South African all-rounder, in his most violent form. Procter scored 155, and in the process hit me to parts of the Oval I had never previously visited. On three traumatic occasions, he stepped outside his leg stump and struck me for six over extra cover off good length, turning balls. The man was impossible.

In desperation, I turned to Jim, hoping to receive some technical instruction from the greatest spinner of the age. 'How the hell would you bowl to Procter when he's in that mood?', I said. Jim considered the problem for a few moments, before delivering a verdict. 'Quite frankly, Percy', he said, 'I wouldn't have a clue.' Other, lesser, men would have offered a stream of worthless platitudes dressed up as guidance. From Jim, I found the comfort of knowing that certain problems have no obvious solution.

But in those early days, I made my way without Jim's advice and I was rather pleased with my progress. At the Oval I discovered new friends and unsuspected cricketing techniques, and in the exotic surroundings of the Orchid Ballroom in Purley, I discovered the lady of my life. It took me all of thirty seconds to tell Diane De Rosa that I was a cricketer; Surrey, actually. She was extremely impressed. Her father was captain of Beddington Seconds, and he had not cared for the string of non-cricketing boy-friends she had been bringing home. Later that evening, she told him she had met a professional

*Jim Laker and Tony Lock
Surrey's legendary spin partnership*

CHAPTER TWO

cricketer, Pat Pocock by name. 'Never heard of him,' said Mr De Rosa. 'He's another one stringing you a line.'

In truth, I did string her a fairly innocuous line by giving her the impression that I was twenty-one years old. Years are desperately important at that period of life, and whereas seventeen seemed callow youth, twenty-one carried the hint of manly experience. Then Surrey spoiled the ploy by selecting me for the first team. I knew that the newspapers would make great play of my age, so I confessed the deception to Diane. She was shocked at exchanging her man of the world for a shambling innocent, and next morning she passed on the news to her mother. It was not a tactful exercise: 'Mum, I've got something to tell you. I don't know how you're going to take it. It's about me and Pat.' Her mother went white. 'You're not . . .? Oh, don't say . . .' Diane spilled out the message in a gabbling rush: 'He's not twenty-one, he's only seventeen, but he *is* a real cricketer and he *does* play for Surrey and they've picked him for the first team and why are you laughing. . .?'

Chapter three

I'll let you have a bouncer in the morning

I HAD read all the stories about Geoffrey Boycott and I wasn't impressed. 'Hate' was the word most often used to describe his approach to the opposition, and the papers made great play of his habit of sitting alone in the dressing room and working up a powerful hatred of the bowling. He had made his debut for England in that year of 1964 and the touring Australians had become the principal targets for his peculiar obsession. This did not worry them unduly, indeed, that sturdy competitor Peter Burge made a point of walking into the England dressing room and saying: "Scuse me, Boycs. Which corner d'you sit in to do your hating?' But that was the reaction of a mature cricketer. For a seventeen-year-old off-spinner, playing in his third championship match, maturity was a distant dream.

Yorkshire were struggling to survive and Boycott had grafted through most of the final afternoon when I got him. The ball turned a little, took an edge, and John Edrich held the catch round the corner. Boycott had to walk down the pitch to pass me on his way out, and I stared at him every step of the way. He stared straight back at me, holding my gaze, and I realised that the stories had been true. I watched him all the way back to the pavilion and I remember thinking; 'You're not the only one who can hate people, Boycott. There's a few of us who can play that game.' I'd begrudged him every run he'd scored, then I'd beaten him and I wanted him to know it. I was still standing and glaring when Roger Harman, our left-arm spinner, came over and put his arm around my shoulder. 'You don't have to do that,' he said. 'You don't have to look at them like that. When you've got them out, you've done them. That's the

23

end of it.' I realised he was right and I've never done it since that day. But it took a while to shake off the feeling, and it took Geoffrey Boycott to bring out that feeling in me.

At this early stage of my career, I was in danger of becoming unbearable. So far, it had all been too easy. I'd taken six wickets off Notts in my first match and in my second I'd dismissed Ted Dexter, captain of England. Ted was not amused. He reached forward, collected the faintest nick and was caught at the wicket. They told me later that he hurled his bat across the Sussex dressing room. 'Fancy getting out to a - - - - colt!,' he shouted. I only wish I could have heard him. Like a boxer who has never been hit, I didn't know enough to be afraid. In that game with Yorkshire, I twice dismissed Brian Close. 'He might have a reputation,' I thought, 'but he's no bother.' My aggression was bubbling over in some disagreeable directions. Keith Fletcher came down the wicket to me in the match with Essex and the ball slid off the toe of his bat and squirted past the leg stump. I swore at him, very loudly, and Micky Stewart sent me across to apologise. 'I'm not having you swearing at batsmen,' he said. 'Well, not at your age.'

If I had a single saving grace, it was an attitude which remained with me through the years: I really thought I could get anybody out. It was the only part of my character which was mature. I knew that there wasn't a player in the game who couldn't give me stick, But I was certain that there wasn't a player I couldn't dismiss.The fact that I was the youngest player for sixty years to make the Surrey first team was a help. Many of the side had been in the second team during the middle and late fifties with no chance of gaining a place in the great side of that era. I knew that some of them resented the ease of my progression to the county side and compared it with their own seasons of hard work and waiting. I also knew that I would have to graft and toil and deliver my share of wickets to justify my existence in their eyes. So I made sure that they could see just how hard I was trying.

If the seniors were finding out about me, then I was making discoveries of my own. This game was a world away from the cheery, beery club cricket experience. There was humour and there was fun, but deep down you were made to realise that these men were playing cricket for a living. Their bread, butter and mortgage repayments depended on how they performed with bat or ball, and, as their colleague, your function was to make that living a little more secure.

It was Ken Barrington who brought the lesson home to me when I walked out to bat for the first time in county cricket in the game against Nottinghamshire. He was on 188 at the time and I was the

Ken Barrington
'The Colonel'

CHAPTER THREE

last man in. 'Are you going to stick around while I get 200?' he asked, doubtfully. 'I'll do my best, Kenny,' I said, and I proceeded to get off the mark with a thick edge off the West Indian Carlton Forbes. That was the last ball I received for the next half-a-dozen overs as Ken nudged and grafted, retained the strike and delivered his double century. The crowd was still applauding the feat when he strolled down the wicket to me: 'OK, son, you can give it a belt now,' he said. 'Great!,' I thought. 'He's got 200, it's my first match and he thinks I should be the one to do the slogging. Thank you very much, Kenny.' But that was his way. He was a little selfish with a bat in his hand but he was a lovely man who was wonderful to play with because he showed you how to be a professional.

Barrington had dissected his own game with extraordinary ruthlessness. He was first picked for England as a shot-maker in the mid-fifties, a player who went for runs and accepted the risks of that approach. The selectors of the time quickly lost patience with him, and they left him out for almost three years while he conducted a reappraisal. He decided that if he cut out seventy-per-cent of his shots, he would reduce the ways of being dismissed by a corresponding proportion, and in the end he was left with a flick off the legs, a cut and, if the ball was pitched right up, an occasional drive. With those three shots he piled up a mountain of runs, but at Surrey we all knew that there was much which was being suppressed. Only two or three times a season would he cut loose and obey his old instincts, then a cry would go up from the dressing room: "Kenny's in the mood!", and we would gather at the window and savour every shot. To witness Barrington in such form was one of the great privileges of playing for Surrey.

My first season coincided with Barrington's benefit year, and, quite naturally, he had worked hard to make the haul as large and as lucrative as possible. He had arranged no fewer than twenty Sunday games, one for every weekend of the season. I played in one of these games at Aldermaston where, on the hottest day of the year, I opened the batting with Stuart Surridge, captain of Surrey's famous team of the fifties. I stayed around for half-an-hour, scored a few runs and came off the field with my shirt dripping with sweat. As I started to search for the showers, I met Ron Tindall, who was awaiting his turn to bat. 'Sorry, Perce,' he said. 'It's only a small ground and there's no showers. But don't worry, they've made arrangements for us to wash in that house over there. Don't go in the front door, use the side door.'

So I picked up my sponge bag and towel, walked down the road to the house and found the room which Ron had described. Unfortunately, there was no shower, so I ran a deep bath and I lay there, singing and soaking, when a stranger put his head round the door. I was slightly surprised that he hadn't knocked before entering, but then, it was his house and gratitude was in order. 'Hallo,' I said. 'The lads told me about the arrangement. Very kind of you.' He didn't seem able to speak. He spluttered quite a bit and shook his head a few times, then he disappeared. I finished my bath and my song, considered borrowing my host's after-shave and strolled back to the cricket ground, impeccably groomed for the evening's entertainment. The first person I met was Tindall. 'Thank you very much,' I said, 'I really needed that bath.' He almost dropped his pint. 'Oh, no,' he said. 'You didn't take me seriously? You didn't really go to a strange house and jump into the bath? Suppose his wife had walked in? Suppose he'd called the police? You must have known I was pulling your leg.' I often wonder if that hospitable stranger has a good memory for faces.

Barrington's principal benefit game was against Yorkshire. It was an inevitable choice since the rivalry between the counties was as bitter as any Test match. Yorkshire was the team we most wanted to beat. Arthur McIntyre would brainwash us with tales of Trueman, Close, Illingworth, John Hampshire and the rest while Micky Stewart, whenever he gave a pep talk, would say: "I don't care if we're playing Glamorgan or Derby, or even Yorkshire . . ." The compliment lay in that 'even'. It was from them that I learned more of the ways of the old pros. Especially from Fred. In my first game against them, Kenny's benefit, I tried to hit Ray Illingworth out of the Oval and succeeded in lifting a skyer, five miles high, to mid-on. Fred was beneath it, turning white and waiting an age for the swirling chance to come down. Everyone in the ground must have heard his sigh of relief when he clung to the ball, but he remembered his status within seconds. 'Ah love them chances', he called across to Illy. 'Easy, them ones.' A year later we played them at Bradford and Fred had plainly marked me down as a rather cocky novice. I batted out the day as night-watchman and I met Fred in the bar that evening. 'You watch yourself, sunshine,' he said. 'Or I'll let you have a bouncer in the morning.' With the innocence of outrageous youth, I took him on. 'Come off it, Fred,' I said. 'You're not quick enough to bowl bouncers these days.' And Trueman snorted. 'Right,' he said, 'It's a promise.' He was as good as his word. First thing next morning, Fred's bouncer reared past my left ear, accompanied by an evil chuckle from the bowler's end. But the point was that he had thought it necessary to warn me first. In later years, I would walk out at Number Eleven and assume that every other ball would be aimed at that same left ear.

CHAPTER THREE

Then, as now, the fast men played their cricket with an aggressive swagger. I remember Jack Flavell's reaction when I got on the front foot to him at Worcester. 'Word of advice, son,' he said in fatherly tones. 'You play forward to me once more, and I'll break your fingers.' Next ball he tried to york me and struck me on the right pad just above the ankle. He received an lbw decision; I received a bruise which ran from ankle to knee. My education was continuing.

But if the learning process was serious, and occasionally painful, the social side of the game offered amusing compensation. Modern cricketers still retain the ability to enjoy themselves after close of play. Indeed, some of the most spectacular parties I have ever attended have been those staged after Test matches abroad. But they are rare occasions. A player may give the bottle a crack for a single night and not touch another drink for perhaps two or three weeks. In the lighter-hearted sixties, with fewer commitments and fewer pressures, the drinker put back four or five pints every night and excelled himself on Saturday evenings with a free day ahead of him. Players would hold court in pubs and pavilions and reel out strings of nostalgic stories, mostly about themselves. Retired players would drift through for beer and memories and even the umpires — invariably the finest raconteurs of all — would be hauled in to make their contributions. Sam Cook, the old Gloucester left-armer, said that spinners were brought up on spin, flight and light ale. After my first two or three seasons, I was still grappling with the mysteries of spin and flight; of light ale there was never a shortage.

On Sundays, players would sleep away their hangovers or dissolve them over eighteen holes. I usually went along with the crowd, then I bought myself a Morris Oxford for £370 and set myself to explore some of the exotic places we were visiting. After one Saturday night session in Nottingham – we stayed at the Black Boy and drank at a gay pub where they used to screw half a crown to the floor and whistle when you stopped to pick it up – I consulted my AA map and decided to drive to Leicester for Sunday lunch. The lads were amazed. 'Do you know?,' they said, 'Percy drove all the way to Leicester for his lunch. *Leicester!*' But I was seventeen, I'd never been there before, and it seemed like a good idea.

The truth was that cricket was resting in a deep, pleasant and extremely comfortable rut. Micky Stewart once told me that thirty per cent of people playing county cricket in the sixties were not really good enough to be performing at that level, and when I look back at the names, I have to agree that he was right. Administrators were divided between those who could see that change was essential and others who regretted the passing of the amateur days and pitched their tents firmly in the thirties. The public was

All in a day's work

apathetic and the game was losing its attraction to the young. I would drive across Clapham Common on summer mornings and see perhaps one match in progress. Ten years later, when the game shed much of its stuffy image, learned to live with one-day cricket and started to give spectators what they actually wanted, I would see ten matches or more taking place on the Common. In the pub in the evening, I would hear ten times as many people talking about cricket. The changes had to arrive, but in those lotus years of the mid-sixties we were far too complacent to see them coming.

We conformed to the leisurely habits of earlier generations. Matches would start at eleven-thirty and we would arrive an hour earlier, read the papers and drink a cup of tea. One or two zealots might go for a net, but most would start changing at ten past eleven, pull on shirt, flannels and boots and bellow: "Come on, lads. Out we go". The thought of fielding practice or exercise never crossed our minds once the season had started, we were there simply to play cricket and we thought we were pretty dedicated fellows. These days, if you're not in the nets by five to ten, they hold an inquest. And if you haven't worked up a sweat by eleven, your place is in serious doubt. Pleasure is optional, results are paramount.

As an established first-team player in my late teens, I was then earning around £1,000 a year. It was a sizeable sum for a carefree single man, but scarcely sufficient for my immediate ambitions. So I took extra jobs, selling fitness training machines at an indoor ski run and paying out punters at Wimbledon dog track, and by March 1966 I had saved enough to marry Diane and buy a flat. She had often wondered how cricket wives coped with their husbands' frequent absences and unsociable hours. Most of all, she wondered how they handled the problem of overseas tours. After seven months of marriage, she was to find out for herself.

Chapter four

He was the kindest, most gentle character in cricket

WHEN the September chill seeps through your second sweater and the paltry crowd has departed by mid-afternoon and the only sound is the umpire's muted yawn as you plod through another over on a pitch as dead as the match itself, that is the time when a cricketer's mind turns to touring. The tour is winter's warm reward for surviving an English winter; week upon week of fine cricket, splendid company and an existence so lavishly pampered that even a lad from suburban Surrey might consider himself a king.

That, at least, was the seductive theory, and I remember pondering it one freezing January evening at the Government Rest House in Sahiwal as I watched them unload the players' beds from the back of a lorry. It was a complicated performance, since several dozen chickens had to be ushered out of the guest rooms before the ancient, wrought-iron structures could be erected. The chickens, as chickens do, had left evidence of their occupation, not only upon the floor but also upon the thin horse-hair mattresses which were draped across the beds. Heating was provided by a small log fire, randomly replenished by a drowsy bearer who would perform the service only after earnest pleading and a handful of rupees. From time to time, a pampered player would rouse himself to complain about the conditions, but it was swiftly pointed out that Pakistan had problems far more pressing than the comfort of tourists and that we were, after all, only an England Under-25 party and could not expect to enjoy the creature comforts of our elders and betters.

I had secured my place on the tour by virtue of eighty-one first-class wickets at twenty-one apiece in my third county season. Our party was of exceptional quality, captained by Mike Brearley and including names like Alan Knott, Dennis Amiss, Derek Underwood, Geoff Arnold, Keith Fletcher and David Brown. In the modern era, with its overseas players limiting the opportunities for young cricketers it would be difficult to select an Under-25 side which was capable of competing for the county championship. Beyond any doubt, that team of 1967 was strong enough to have challenged for the title. Yet the punishing schedule and primitive conditions combined to extend even that remarkably talented side to its limits. When we were not playing, we were travelling. And when we spilled off our plane or train or overnight coach, there was always a reception to be attended, speeches to endure and toasts to our hosts to be drunk in warm fruit juice.

The low points were the lowest I ever experienced on any cricket tour. I remember visiting Amiss when he collapsed with chronic diarrhoea and leaving him to lie on that horse-hair mattress whilst he contemplated another spate of short singles. I remember too the room-service at the appalling hotel in Dacca when I ordered tea on a blistering afternoon. The bearer arrived with a rusty tray, and as he put the tea on the table, a huge cockroach scuttled out of my bed. He was on to the monster in a flash, squashed it in his hand and casually tossed the carcass into the corridor. I glanced at the milk jug and saw that the liquid carried a coating of thick green slime. Not unreasonably, I asked for fresh milk. The bearer nodded his assent, and proceeded to wash out the jug with hands which still bore vivid memories of the deceased cockroach.

It was too much, even for the strongest stomach. Alan Knott's stomach was weaker than most. I scarcely knew the man before that tour; by the time six weeks had passed, I revered him as one of the most endearing eccentrics the game has produced. Knotty's life was devoted to the single-minded pursuit of cleanliness. Good health was his obsessive ambition, and it was only to be achieved by constant exercise, ceaseless vigilance and the waging of a relentless war against predatory germs. For Alan Knott, Pakistan was the front line in that conflict. When he dressed in the morning, he made quite sure that he carried a pen in the pocket of his shirt. In this way, he would not have to risk infectious contact with alien pens while signing autographs. He also went to extraordinary lengths to avoid shaking strange hands; more contact, more risk. We used to bribe passing fans to offer him their hands, with the promise of more rupees if they were successful. Knotty would wriggle and squirm and thrust his hands deep into his pockets. He told them that in his country, when strangers were introduced, the custom was to smile and wink. One of the most amazing sights of the entire trip was Knotty's face, creased into a chilling grimace with one eye winking

Alan Knott . . . one of the most endearing eccentrics the game has produced

furiously while friendly locals attempted to tug his hands from his pockets.

His habits grew increasingly bizarre, and his suspicion of the sub-continent was not allayed, even when we stayed at a first-class hotel. I once watched him order afternoon tea from room service. It was a memorable ceremony: 'I would like a pot of tea for two and another pot of hot water, please' — somebody had told him that strong tea was bad for the stomach. 'And do you have honey? Excellent. And some jam, please. Nothing wrong with jam.' And in it would come on a linen doyly, an elegant feast. Knotty would then go to the bathroom and pull out half-a-dozen tissues, which he would use to clean out the cups, saucers, knives and spoons. He would then shake up the sugar to make sure it was fresh and dust down the jam jars and tray. The butter would be resting on a bed of ice. This did not escape Knotty's attention. Off he would go for fresh tissues — he could not, of course, use the same one twice — and pat away all the tiny globules of water which adhered to the butter. He had heard that the water was dangerous and he was taking no chances.

If Pakistan represented the front line in Knotty's war, then the rest of the planet offered the chance for minor skirmishes. Occasionally, we would go to a respected London restaurant where Knotty would confound the wine waiter by ordering 'weak tea.' When the insipid solution was delivered, he would reach under the table and emerge with a pot of honey because he had heard that honey was good for you. For reasons which may have become obvious, we called him 'Alan Nut,' and over the years I became a student of his eccentricities. He once bought an old van and fitted it with an orthopaedic chair — 'very good for the back.' He would strap a house brick onto his brake pedal to take some of the strain out of braking and he would always drive with a soft deerstalker hat on to prevent head colds. His cars, naturally, were invariably fitted with automatic transmission, since gear changing was so bad for the achilles tendon. Like all the best eccentrics, he was quite impervious to ridicule. Where other players might take ten minutes to pack a bag, Knotty would set aside anything up to five hours for the task; adjusting his toilet bag, re-arranging his shirts and musing endlessly on the best way to lay out his wicket-keeping gloves. I have known him have a meal sent up to his room so that he would not have to walk downstairs and upset the essential rhythm of packing. Yet with all this, he was the kindest, most gentle character in cricket. He rated everybody, never uttered an unkind criticism and revelled in the successes of his colleagues. Even when he staggered me with his fads and fussiness, I loved him like a brother.

In truth, the tour badly needed the distraction which Knotty's antics provided. It was, in retrospect, the least enjoyable excursion of my career. The results were entirely acceptable in that we won four and drew three of the seven games against tenacious opposition. There was also the pleasure of playing under the calculating captaincy of Mike Brearley and the additional pleasure of watching him strike what may have been the finest batting form of his life; he averaged 132 from nine innings and took a breathtaking triple-century in a day off North Zone at Peshawar. I was pleased with my own contribution as I finished as a leading wicket-taker with thirty-one at twenty apiece and learned a lot about bowling at technically adept batsmen on unfriendly wickets. And yet, curiously, I was disappointed by the entire experience. I had heard the old pros hold court for an entire evening with their tales of touring. All I could show for my first overseas trip was a sore spinning finger, a tour fee of £300 and a small fund of hotel horror stories.

We finished the tour with a brief bout of luxury at the International Hotel in Lahore. We dined with the British High Commissioner and were treated like royalty on the long flight home. Two days later I began a six-week stint driving lorries for a haulage company. Diane was a secretary with the British Railways Board and we would meet after work and return to our little flat in Wallington where we would dine off fish and chips. As a way of life, it may have been mundane, but I never thought it so. For I was a well-travelled man of nineteen. And I had seen the Government Rest House at Sahiwal.

Chapter five

If I tell him all my secrets, he'll finish up pinching my place

IT WAS Tom Graveney who put into words what many of the England players were thinking. 'You're twenty-one years old, you're the junior pro, you're still soaking wet behind the ears and you've got a sight too much to say for yourself', he said. 'Now do us all a favour and keep quiet.'

A wiser man might have heeded the reprimand from such an esteemed professional, but I treated it as an irksome inconvenience. I had survived the ordeal of Pakistan, I had accumulated one hundred and twelve wickets in the 1967 season and here I was, staring across the waters of Montego Bay in the company of the finest cricketers of the generation and living out all my touring fantasies. Perhaps Tom was right, perhaps I should have curbed my precocious chattering. But perhaps he had forgotten how it felt to be twenty-one years old and to see your ambitions moving into sharper focus. The Pakistan tour had been crammed with excellent players; this West Indian expedition seemed to be staffed almost exclusively by gods. It was probably the last occasion on which England was able to send abroad so many players of authentic greatness. I used to look at the team list and shake my head at the wonder of it all: Geoffrey Boycott, John Edrich, Colin Cowdrey, Ken Barrington, Tom Graveney. If you were picking the best, most gifted England batting line-up of all time, you might not look too far past those first five players. When you add the talents of Basil d'Oliveira, Alan Knott, Jim Parks, Fred Titmus and, subsequently, Tony Lock, plus the pace of John Snow, David Brown and Jeff Jones, you will understand our conviction that we had a team equipped to take on all comers.

In retrospect, 'team' is a somewhat misleading description of the group which toured the West Indies in 1968. There was a strong whiff of self-interest in the air, with the older players fighting to protect their reputations and the young ones striving, without tact or shame, to cast a few shadows of their own. The one thing which unified these clashing egos and conflicting ambitions was the streak of selfish pride, common to the best English professionals, which drove them to perform their own tasks to the limit of their talent. As captain, Cowdrey presided over his unpredictable crew with gentle diffidence. A charming man, possessed of a sublime talent, he was the least forceful of leaders. He shunned controversy, avoided confrontation and genuinely believed that all his players shared his own standards of responsibility. His faith was not always justified.

His vice-captain, Fred Titmus, spent much of the early part of the tour struggling with his own form. I had always admired Fred as a massively accomplished off-spinner, a man who could bowl to any batsman on any surface. I had also entertained vague hopes that Fred might, as the weeks went by, pass on a few of the mysteries of his art to this wide-eyed lad. Fred was civil and friendly, but he was yet another canny old pro. His attitude was: 'If I tell him all my secrets, he'll finish up pinching my place. Let him find out for himself.' There was no animosity about it, we both understood the position, and I was as upset as anybody when Fred suffered the freak boating accident which prematurely terminated his trip.

John Snow was to emerge as a truly important Test bowler on that tour, and his was an amazing triumph of talent over attitude. He had made that attitude abundantly clear at our pre-tour net practice at Crystal Palace, where he turned up an hour late and demonstrated his disdain for the exercise by bowling left-handed. Full-hearted commitment had never been his style. He would try for Sussex only when he felt the occasion merited his efforts, and you always sensed that county cricket was rather beneath him. Yet he was the most accurate fast bowler I ever played against. He didn't really need to practice, he would simply stroll out, settle into his groove and bowl line and length to order. His major flaw had been his habit of bowling everything into the batsman, every delivery would be pushed or swung down the same line. But his break-through in the West Indies was achieved by his discovery of what he called "away-swinging arse balls", a typically vivid description of the small adjustment to his action which brought his rear end round, set him sideways on to the batsman and produced a fast and deceptive out-swinger. He became almost childishly excited by the novelty of the delivery, so much so that he would practice it through long sessions in the nets. He could sense that he was on the verge of becoming an outstanding pace bowler, and the thought appealed to him.

Boycott, of course, could not understand any cricketer who did not believe that God had created the hours of daylight for the exclusive purpose of net practice. He did not care for Snow, whom he referred to as 'Prima'. Geoffrey never could understand people who insisted on having things their own way, especially when their way clashed with his, and the friction between the two grew to the point where Tom Graveney had to step between them during a dressing room row in mid-tour. My first encounter with Boycott had been that long exchange of stares at the Oval, but I began to know him a little better after rooming with him for a couple of weeks early in the tour. Rooming with Boycott is a very serious event in a cricketer's life. You are quickly made to realise that you have come to this distant country on business. The thought of enjoyment should not enter your mind, since it never entered his. He attended receptions resentfully and left them early so that he could get back to the room and think about the runs he was going to score and the extra time he was going to spend in the nets and who he could get to bowl to him and how he could improve an average which was increasing with every innings. He spoke only of cricket or Yorkshire, since the two things in his mind were synonymous. He spoke, and you listened as that quiet, flat-vowelled voice droned on into the night; it was the voice of a middle-aged man in his mid-twenties, the voice of a man who had never been young. I had never encountered such dedication, and I found myself feeling a little sorry for his contemporaries who had designs on his England place. They brought a normal, competitive approach to their cricket, and I knew beyond question that their approach would never have a chance against his consuming obsession.

Yet for all his grim intensity, there were some strangely endearing aspects of that complex personality, and there was one trait of his which always surprised me. When, reluctantly, he finished net practice for the day, he would invariably seek out and thank each of the bowlers who had provided that practice. If one bowler had been taken out of the net before the end and sent to a fielding practice on the other side of the ground, Boycott would trudge across in his pads, shake the helping hand and say: "Thanks very much. You bowled for half an hour and it's hot out here and I appreciate what you've done for me." A small gesture, perhaps, but you found yourself weighing it in the balance when you heard other, less flattering stories about this extraordinary man.

As his opening partner, John Edrich was a player who was entering his prime. He was a seasoned pro and one of the best of his breed, but the charge of selfishness could never be laid at his door. He was probably the least selfish great player I ever knew. I was to play alongside him for fifteen years, and I never saw him play for himself, never saw him hog soft bowling or try to lose strike in the final over. I also never knew a great player who thought less about the technicalities of the game, which was one of the factors which was to make him such a poor county captain. He believed cricket to be the simplest game in the world and he played it accordingly. He would increase his repertoire by one shot every five years. When he started, he used to cut and drive on the off-side and he had a walking shot, back foot ahead of front, which allowed him to flip the ball over mid-wicket. In the manner of Ken Barrington, he scored thousands of runs with those three shots, and only slowly did his on-side game come into play. His temperament was not only admirable, but possibly unique. He could play and miss the first five balls of an over and shape up for the sixth as if it were the first delivery of the day. 'They can only bowl one ball at a time', he used to say. 'When they start bowling two, that's when I'll start worrying.' The prospect of facing Hall and Griffith left him serenely unruffled, in fact he was far more concerned with the problems involved in organising his benefit season at home. He had a friend on the telephone exchange who allowed him free calls to the United Kingdom, and he would spend hours every week on the phone in his room. He may not have given his cricket an excessive amount of thought, but when it came to business, John Edrich never missed a trick.

I was fascinated by the entire scene, and in particular by the relationships between the players. Boycott ploughed his own po-faced furrow as he set about piling up 1,154 tour runs in a convincing attempt to prove himself a great player. Barrington was a different man on tour, more withdrawn and less friendly than the engaging character I knew at Surrey. Ken Higgs, the Lancashire medium-pacer, was thoroughly miserable throughout, never came to terms with his failure to make the Test side and frequently took out his frustration on Colin Cowdrey, who was far too gentle ever to take serious offence. Colin Milburn arrived in the Caribbean with a reputation as a crowd-pleaser. He did not let his public down. On every island, they singled him out for special applause and when we reached Trinidad, they persuaded him to enter a calypso contest with The Mighty Sparrow, who had reigned virtually unchallenged as Calypso King. Olly Milburn rose to the occasion, belted out 'The Green, Green Grass of Home" and won such applause that the Sparrow, who saw his crown slipping away, ushered him off the stage. Everybody loved Olly, a fact which seemed to irritate Tom Graveney. Tom was the player of real quality, yet he was being overshadowed in the public eye by an exciting striker who lacked

CHAPTER FIVE

Tom's pedigree. He tended to pick on Olly, singling him out for carping criticism. It was a curious reaction from a man whose own reputation was unassailable.

Meanwhile, I continued to chatter in spite of Graveney's pointed advice. I don't think I was conceited, but I was certainly very happy. I had won my Surrey cap a few months earlier, I was mixing on roughly equal terms with some of the finest cricketers the game had ever seen and, the conventional wisdom insisted, I was at least ten years away from my peak as a spinner. My happiness was excusable, less so my naiveté. I still squirm when I think of the cars I drove in Trinidad and the effect they had upon the senior players.

There was a wealthy man on the island whose delight was to throw lavish parties for visiting sportsmen. It was at one of these affairs that I was offered the use of an extremely large Cadillac. I accepted with pleasure, and spent rest days screaming around the roads of that delightful haven in this enormous beast. I had just enough tact to park it at the back of the hotel, away from the eyes of the Press and senior pros, but in the end I was spotted. I bumped into Graveney as he queued for a taxi. 'Got yourself a car, I hear', he said. 'A big car, too. Very nice for you, I'm sure.' And he didn't sound as if he meant it.

But by now I was into my stride. The team had been given the use of two cars, a Ford Corsair and a Ford Zephyr. As captain, Cowdrey monopolised the Corsair, while the Zephyr was handed to our manager, Les Ames. Now the Zephyr's gear box was an unsynchronised wreck and neither Les nor any of the senior players could fathom its workings. Enter the junior pro, with the precious experience of having driven a four-ton Thames Trader for the haulage company at home. By now I had handed back the Cadillac, and I had the nerve to ask the manager for the use of his car. As I was the only player able to drive the heap, he could scarcely refuse. I would leave it in second gear whenever he needed it, and in that solitary gear he would travel to and from the cricket ground. But for the rest of the time, it was mine, and my elders would watch me sweep out to dinner, crashing ostentatiously through the Zephyr's gears while they begged lifts from mobile strangers.

I played my trump card just before the first Test match, when the hospitable party-giver insisted that I borrow his own car, a large, bright red, three-litre Aston Martin. It was madness to accept the invitation, but I did, and you could almost hear the hiss of resentment as I roared up to the hotel in that ferocious machine.

It was Basil d'Oliveira who spoke up for me. In fact, the more outrageous I became, the more staunchly he defended me. 'Leave him alone', he would say. 'He's twenty-one years old. If he's not

*John Edrich . . .
the least selfish great player I ever knew*

CHAPTER FIVE

going to enjoy life now, when will he enjoy it?' I thought the world of Basil, and not just because he was my defender. He attacked life the way he attacked his cricket, he was still a young pro at heart with all the gleeful faults of youth, and he dismissed the hard-bitten postures of the seniors. Basil was great for the game, the kind of man who would come in on a hat-trick and drive you for a straight six. Ian Botham was still a decade away, yet Basil was carrying his standard in that England side. Unfortunately, he was also giving the booze a considerable crack. He was the worse for wear on one or two social occasions and the resulting publicity did not improve his image in the eyes of distant Lord's. But he cared little for image. He careered around the islands intent upon enjoyment, and the junior pro was his willing accomplice. I remember leaving an official reception with Basil one evening in Montego Bay. We jumped into a taxi, an ancient Consul, and we were humming along the highway when Basil grunted: 'How much are you going to charge us, then?' I realised that he had drunk deeply because he was talking through his teeth, as he did on such occasions. The Jamaican taxi driver glanced over his shoulder and mumbled: 'Fifteen dollars.' Two seconds later, the driver was sitting in the back seat between us, Basil having reached forward and dragged him out of the front. Nobody was driving the car. I was terrified. I leaned forward, grabbed the wheel and attempted to keep us on the road. All the time I was yelling: 'Basil! You idiot! What made you do that?' He ignored me to concentrate upon the driver. 'How much did you say?', he asked. 'How much?' The driver explained that he had mistaken us for American tourists, that the real fare was six dollars and would Basil kindly put him back in the front seat. Eventually he did, and the man continued on his way, shaking like a leaf. Basil sat and stared out of the window. 'American tourists', he kept saying. 'Us American tourists. Can you believe it?' Controversy always surrounded Basil, and much of it, as you may gather, he brought down on his own head. Yet he remained an immensely popular man whose qualities far out-numbered his aberrations.

If England could assemble a whole constellation of superb players, then the West Indies could counter them talent for talent. The list has grown no less daunting with the years: Nurse, Camacho, Kanhai, Butcher, Lloyd, Sobers, Holford, Murray, Griffith, Hall and Gibbs. It is best not to linger over such a collection, best to speak their names quickly and hope that the day will not find them in their meanest mood. Personally, I expected to play no real part in the major conflicts, since Titmus was the established and accomplished off-spinner. But I was pleased just to be a part of the supporting cast, to do my work in the island matches, to bowl countless overs in the nets, to dry their shirts and fetch their meals and bring their drinks and generally act like a willing lackey. The memories remain vivid and stunning; Kenny Barrington smoking an endless stream of cigarettes before walking out to face Charlie Griffith in the First Test at Port of Spain. Kenny had had the nerve to say publicly what the whole world of cricket recognised privately, that Griffith was a chucker, that his bouncer and yorker were deliberate throws and that he should have been banned from Test cricket. This was their first Test match meeting since the allegation had been made, and 25,000 Trinidadians made sure that Kenny knew what was in store as he came down the pavilion steps. 'Char-lie! Char-lie!', they chanted with every stride, and Griffith responded with a performance of fearsome hostility. Kenny ducked and weaved, he was struck on back and shoulder but the old Surrey pro won that opening battle by grafting six and a half hours for 143 out of an English total of 568, and only a late and patient stand between Gary Sobers and Wes Hall saved an innings defeat and carried West Indies to a draw.

The Second Test in Kingston produced my first experience of the ugly violence which was to disfigure all too many of my subsequent tours.

England were in comfortable command until mid-afternoon on the third day when Jim Parks took a diving leg-side catch to dismiss Basil Butcher. Suddenly the bottles began to fly from the boundary and explode upon the pitch. Colin Cowdrey pleaded bravely and uselessly for order, but then the police and riot squads over-reacted in the grand manner and cleared the ground in minutes. I sat and marvelled at the amazing throwing arms of the Jamaican fans, for the bottles continued to reach the middle of the pitch from outside the ground. Then I saw the clouds of tear gas drift across the field and burn the eyes and mouths of the entire pavilion. They called off play for the day, added seventy-five minutes to an extra sixth day and from a position of domination, England collapsed against the spin of Sobers and Gibbs, securing a draw with just two wickets in hand.

The next two weeks altered the course of my career. We played Barbados in Bridgetown on a wicket so perfect that Boycott contributed 243 to a total of 578 for five declared. On that same perfect wicket, against a side containing Sobers, Nurse, Holford and Peter Lashley, I took five for 48 off forty-one overs. Boycott to his credit, nagged at me throughout the spell offering exactly the right advice: 'Keep concentrating', he would say. 'Keep concentrating, Perce.' I knew my performance had made an impression, especially when Tom Graveney, who was then no great supporter of mine, announced that he had just witnessed the finest passage of off-spin bowling since the days of Jim Laker. Then poor Fred Titmus lost his toes in that gruesome accident on the rest day before the Third Test. He was clinging to the side of a motorboat driven by Penny Cowdrey when his foot became caught in the propeller which was situated in the middle of the hull. Four toes were sliced off and Fred's tour had ended. In later years we would hand him some tasteless stick over that accident: 'What's got six toes and spins? Fred Titmus.' But it was a shattering blow, for it seemed that a brilliant career had died on that February day in Barbados.

Yet even as we sat by his hospital bed and sympathised, the implications were obvious. We had lost our Test off-spinner, we were on the eve of the Third Test match and I had just bowled better than I had ever bowled in my life. I waited for Cowdrey to read out the team, and I knew that the choice was inevitable. 'Surrey and England', I kept thinking. 'Surrey and England. Who would have thought it?' And then a telegram arrived from England and I knew it was really happening. Jim Laker had sent his best wishes.

*St Vincent, West Indies . . .
the simple, superb setting which expresses all the charm
and vitality of West Indian cricket*

*Queen's Park Oval, Port of Spain, Trinidad . . .
Site of more than one famous English victory
and the venue for Sir Gary Sobers' final Test match*

Chapter six

We'll keep a welcome in the hillside

A FEW years ago during a particularly unsuccessful England tour, an elderly member of MCC walked through the team hotel and shook his head in disapproval. 'Too many wives,' he declared. 'Time was when a chap went away for six months, ruined his marriage and won the Test series. This lot bring their wives with them, save their marriages and lose every Test match.'

A few traces of that neanderthal view still survived in 1968, and I could sense the disapproval in certain quarters when Diane came out to join me in Barbados. Wives were still something of a rarity on tour, submissive creatures to be left at home to run the house, bring up the children and prepare for the hero's return. I had little time for that attitude. As soon as the tour selection was announced, I visited a small terraced house in North London where I met the Secretary of the Trinidad and Tobago Friends Association. From my tour fee of £700, I handed over £105 to make Diane a member of that Association and secure her place on their charter flight to the West Indies. It was not the easiest journey; four hours to the Azores and fifteen hours to Trinidad on an ancient Britannia, followed by an island hop to Barbados. But her timing was perfect and she arrived just a few days before my Test match debut. Unfortunately, my arrangements for her accommodation were less than tactful. On the team's first visit to Barbados, I had met a cricketer named Arthur Bethell. He heard that Diane was coming out, he lived just a mile down the road from the England team hotel and he invited her to stay with his family. Just before she arrived, he called to say that he was taking a holiday. 'But don't worry,' he said. 'Here's the house, here's the car, these are the servants and this is our beach. Make yourself at home.' I then had to approach Colin Cowdrey and ask if he would mind my staying out of the team hotel. 'It's only a mile away,' I said, 'but don't worry, I've got a car.' Now at this stage of the tour, even the captain did not possess a car. But he swallowed hard and gave the junior pro his permission, on condition that I arrived early enough to take breakfast with the team every morning and thus concealed my nocturnal absences from the Press. I relished my days of incomparable luxury, but, looking back, I cringe at my cavalier behaviour. The prejudice of the senior players was spectacularly reinforced and, with the hindsight of the years, I can well understand their feelings.

Tom Graveney may well have had that episode in mind when we strolled across the Bridgetown ground on the day before the Test. 'See that sightscreen?' he said. 'Last time I played here, that screen was peppered with little red dots where Clyde Walcott had got after Jim Laker. Oh yes, they love off-spinners on this ground.' And off he walked, smiling wickedly. But the crack was quickly forgotten in the excitement of the hour. All the cricket I had ever played had been a preparation for this moment. All of history's great players had known the agony of anticipation which I was enduring. I was determined to enjoy the experience.

In the event, mine was a protracted introduction to Test cricket. The West Indies batted first and batted ponderously. Although there were interruptions for rain, they occupied the crease until mid-morning on the third day for their 349. And yet, in the kindly words of Wisden, I had bowled 'steadily and intelligently'. My twenty-eight overs had cost fifty-five runs, and my reward had been the wicket of Clive Lloyd. It was an unusual success for one who was always a poor fielder to his own bowling. I can remember flighting the ball, holding it back a shade and trembling as Lloyd gave it the kitchen sink with his drive. In the next day's papers, there was a picture of me bent over backwards like a banana and clutching the ball in front of my chin. Many years later, Lloyd was to admit that he thought he had hit that ball hard enough to have drilled it through me. My instinct for self-preservation had given me my first Test wicket.

My other enduring memory of that drawn game was of batting for more than an hour with John Snow one morning. The new ball had been taken and handed first to Wes Hall and then Charlie Griffith, the fastest bowlers in the world. Not once in that hour was I required to duck. Now that could not happen today. At their speed and in that situation, I would accept that my head was at the mercy of the West Indian attack. But I was a tail-ender, there was a code that we should not receive bouncers and that code was obeyed without question. The game still carried a few humanitarian trappings.

In common with the other English bowlers, I suffered some stern punishment in the West Indies second innings when Lloyd began to swing the bat to appalling effect, but I felt that at last I was being treated seriously. That pre-Test performance in Barbados had provoked a re-assessment of my ability and there was a growing feeling in the camp that the junior pro might actually have something to contribute to the tour. Then they sent for Tony Lock.

They tracked down the old chap in a bar in Tasmania and told him that England expected him as soon as possible. Typically, he took his time to arrive; via Hobart, Sydney, Perth and all the hops to London before crossing the Atlantic to Trinidad. I was furious. I had been taken on the tour as second off-spinner. I had performed reasonably well when my chance arrived and now I was about to be overlooked in favour of a man who had been discarded. Cowdrey had the decency to explain the decision, taking me aside to tell me that our close catching was letting us down, that chances were going to ground all too often and that the selectors were placing their faith in the best close catcher of his generation. I was still mulling over this reasoning as I drifted through the lobby of the Queen's Park Hotel in Port of Spain one morning when I heard a familiar voice bellowing my name. 'Percy!,' came the cry, and Lock strode over from the reception desk to shake my hand. The lovable rogue had worked wonders at Leicestershire during the previous season in England. He was acting as the resident mercenary for Western Australia and now, as if it were the most natural progression that one could imagine, he had flown around the world to play a Test match for England. The senior pros were delighted at this resuscitation of a trusted old sweat. 'Locky's here,' they would say. 'Now we can get stuck into this lot.' I found myself admiring his style and the nonchalance with which he took everything in his stride. But for the first and, thankfully, the only time in my career, I wanted to see a fellow professional fail.

I wasn't proud of that reaction, for even in my short career I had come to cherish Lock as one of the game's glorious eccentrics. He was, as I came to realise, slightly mad. During his years with Surrey, he had a curious passion for cowboy books, and I suspect that many of his theatrical gestures had their roots in those pages. When Surrey were batting, he would put his pads on early so that he could sit undisturbed with his tales of the Old West. Once, when the team was chasing runs, Lock spent the entire innings wrapped up in his latest epic. Suddenly the call came: 'You're in.' He stood up, marked his place in the book, looked around for his bat and inquired: 'How many do we need?' They told him that five runs were required.

*John Snow . . .
an amazing
triumph of talent
over attitude*

*Tom Graveney . . .
his public grace and elegance
were achieved at the cost of enormous mental stress*

CHAPTER SIX

'Right,' he said, in the manner of his Western heroes. 'In that case. I shall hit a six.' And he did, off the first ball. In all his years of cricket, his character never changed. Sam Cook of Gloucestershire once told me that he had played in Lock's second championship match. He saw an eighteen-year-old with a shock of ginger hair walking to the wicket and he asked the non-striking Surrey batsman, Jack Parker, about him. 'Promising lad,' he was told. 'Name's Tony Lock. Quite a useful bowler.' Sam flighted his first ball at Lock, who lifted it into the back of the pavilion. As the ball screamed through the air, the teenager shouted down the wicket to his partner: 'Come - - - - - six!'

Along with the arrogant aggression, there was a strange vulnerability about the man. The harder he tried to impress, the more likely were his efforts to end in farce. Micky Stewart loved to tell how he and his wife Sheila were once summoned to dinner with Lock in Leicester. He greeted them at the Grand Hotel, asked permission to smoke during the first course and somehow contrived to scatter an entire box of matches in his soup. As he entertained the Stewarts, he studied the wine list, unable to make up his mind. Three times the wine waiter came to the table for his order, and three times he was told that Mr Lock was still undecided. Mid-way through the main course, the waiter made a fourth approach. 'Come on, Locky,' said Micky. 'You've got to order something soon.' Lock gave the list one last, long stare. 'All right,' he said, as he snapped shut the book. And he ordered with a single word: 'Red!' Dinner seemed to bring the worst out of Lock. He had been on the West Indian tour for scarcely a week when he went with Robin Hobbs for an Indian meal in Guyana. The meal did not please him. Indeed, he complained that the curry was too mild. A few days later, the pair returned to the same restaurant where Lock demanded the hottest curry in the house. He took a mouthful, picked up the plate, hurled it across the room and watched the inadequate curry slide down the restaurant wall. 'That was clever,' said Hobbs. 'Very clever, that was.' Lock was unmoved, just like the gunfighters of his books. 'When I say hot,' he drawled, 'hot is what I mean.'

Aside from his curry-throwing habits, I had nothing against this outrageous character, but, for my own reasons of injured pride, I wanted to see him fail in the Fourth Test. The West Indies compiled 526 for seven declared in their first innings and Lock was carted around the Queen's Park Oval for the damaging figures of one for 129 off thirty-two overs. His suffering did not end with his bowling. The man who had been brought in to improve our close-catching spilled two chances between his knees. Shamefully, I was rather pleased to see them go down. Yet I remained fiercely loyal to the side and I was delighted at the outlandish turn which the match was to take.

England responded to that huge West Indian total with a first innings score of 414, largely due to a masterly 148 from Cowdrey. Gary Sobers then made a declaration for which some West Indians have yet to forgive him. With Griffith out of the game with an injured leg, Sobers called off his men at ninety-two for two and invited us to score 215 in two and three-quarter hours for victory. Although he played no part in the run-chase, it was Barrington who made our success possible. After a quiet start and the loss of a couple of wickets, the tea-time dressing room was uncertain of the wisdom of pursuing the target. Then up spoke Kenny, the cautious, pragmatic percentage player. 'Will we go for it?,' he yelled. 'Of course we'll go for it! That's what we've come all this way for, isn't it?' The decision was made. Cowdrey and Boycott went out and played all their shots and England came home with three minutes and seven wickets to spare.

One up with one to play, the common expectation was that England would select the same eleven players to protect their lead. But there was a complication. We were aware that the pitch in Guyana would take spin and the temptation was to leave out one of the three pace men in order to play a second spinner. I had one more chance to state my case and I took six for fifty-seven in the second innings of the island game with Guyana. Two days later, Lock responded with five for thirty-six in the one-day match with Guyana Colts. The combination was unresolved, and remained so until an hour before the start of play on the morning of the final Test. It was then that I endured one of the most humiliating experiences of my entire career.

I was summoned to a net at the Border ground, where I found Colin Cowdrey, Kenny Barrington, Tom Graveney and Tony Lock waiting by the side of the wicket. Cowdrey spoke on their behalf. 'We have only ever seen you bowl in an attacking fashion,' he said. 'We don't know if you can bowl it flat ánd keep it tight.' He then tossed a batting glove on the wicket and informed me that my Test place that day depended upon the number of times that I could pitch the ball on or close to that glove. I was shocked. This was the way an insensitive coach might have treated a raw colt. It was not the way to select an England side. For a few seconds I considered telling them precisely what they could do with their batting glove, but ambition overcame me. I wanted to play in the Test and if that was what I had to do to get a game, then so be it. So I concentrated on bowling around two dozen balls at that glove, eliminating my usual loop and firing them in flat and fast. Sometimes I hit it, sometimes I brushed

CHAPTER SIX

it. People strolling past the net on their way to the match must have wondered what these mad Englishmen were cooking up. But my performance seemed to satisfy my jury. There was a short, mumbled conversation and Cowdrey's face broke into a smile. 'All right,' he said. 'You're in'. Naturally, I was delighted, but deep down the humiliation rankled. So far as I am aware, my trial by jury was unique in the history of Test cricket. For the sake of the game's dignity, I trust it will remain so.

After an experience like that, the match itself could have proved almost an anti-climax. In fact, it developed into a classic among cliff-hangers. The West Indies first innings saw Sobers make elegant amends for his premature declaration in Trinidad by stroking 152 of their 414 total. My attempts to reproduce my morning net form were reasonably successful. Although I took only one wicket, the cost of my 38 overs was just seventy-eight. Then Boycott put together another hundred for us, his fourth of the tour, before the middle order collapsed and we stood at 259 for eight. I then came out to join Lock, who started to lay about the bowling with some success. Our partnership was a trifle one-sided, in that it took me eighty-two minutes to get off the mark. In the history of Test cricket only Godfrey Evans had waited longer. But I stayed there while Lock battered everything they served up to him. We were still there with 93 between us overnight, Lock's share being 76 and extras making a sporting contribution, and we carried it to 109 on the morning of the fifth day, a record ninth-wicket partnership for England against West Indies. I made thirteen, Lock scored 89 and with England finishing on 371 the selectors were congratulating themselves on the wise selection of two spinners.

But Sobers, inevitably, had still more to offer. He played another chanceless and beautiful innings before running out of partners just five runs short of his hundred. The proposition could not have been plainer. England needed to score 308 to win or, more realistically, bat throughout the sixth and final day in order to draw the game and win the series. After the first ninety-five minutes, the Georgetown crowd had already started to celebrate the imminence of a famous West Indian victory. We had lost five wickets for forty-one runs and the toil and graft of the past three and a half months was about to be squandered. Then Cowdrey and Knott came together and sanity returned. Cowdrey played with massive assurance and on that day Knott was his equal. Together they put on 127 and when the captain went for 82, Knott was left with the task of protecting the tail-enders for the last seventy minutes. He lost John Snow, then Lock departed and I came in praying that I might stick it out until the end. As it was, a kind of poetic justice caught up with me. Lance Gibbs bowled me a quick ball outside off-stump. I flashed at it and got the faintest of faint edges. Of the entire West Indian side, clustered around the bat, only the wicket keeper Deryck Murray went up in appeal. Now there were only a couple of occasions in my career when I declined to walk when I knew I had nicked the ball, and this was one of them. 'I'm not going for that,' I thought. 'That's much too fine an edge.' So I stayed in and the umpire's finger stayed down. With the next ball, Gibbs bowled me a full toss, an attempted yorker. I played it into the ground and Clive Lloyd, fielding in front of the bat, caught it on the bounce, threw it miles in the air, performed a war dance and screeched an appeal. Up went the finger.

As I walked off, I passed Jeff Jones on his way in. Jeff, as the whole of Glamorgan could tell you, was the ultimate non-batsman. He scarcely knew which end of the bat to hold. He was not, frankly, a man who inspired confidence in his ability to survive the two remaining overs. I reached the dressing room and feared the worst. Cowdrey, Barrington and Lock were of like mind, for they had all retreated to the lavatory where they occupied traps one, two and three and waited for the bad news. Knott played out the penultimate over but could not force the single to give himself strike. By now, Jeff was trembling. The Welshman knew his limitations and knew that Gibbs, the world's finest spinner, was about to bowl him an over which would decide the series. As he prepared for his ordeal, he looked up and saw Knott sauntering down the wicket towards him. Knott didn't say a word, he simply leaned forward and sang a couple of bars of 'We'll keep a welcome in the hillside'. Jones smiled, some of his tension evaporated and, with an intense effort of will, he kept out the six remaining balls to give England the series.

We held a small dressing room celebration but reserved our real energies for the long night ahead. After all the problems and all the crises, there was much to celebrate. I was wandering away from the ground with Snow and Lock, when handfuls of small pebbles started to fall at our feet. They were followed by larger stones, then by a steel chair which struck and cut the lad who was carrying our bags. A large crowd had now gathered as we ran to our car and a police car, reversing at improbable speed, cleared a path for us. Mounted police were charging the crowd and again we were held up by rioters. Lock was bleeding badly from a head wound and the situation was almost beyond control when we saw a gap, hurtled through it and screamed off to the safety of the hotel. I remember slumping in the back seat, speechless with fear. For once, the junior pro had nothing to say for himself. It had taken three and a half marvellous months, but, at last, Tom Graveney's advice had been accepted.

Chapter seven

I've already worked him out. But don't go telling the others

THE letter was couched in the gentle terms I would have expected from Colin Cowdrey, and its sentiments were sympathetic. 'Please don't be too downhearted,' he wrote, 'and don't read too much into this selection. Your day will come.' I received it with mixed feelings. Not too many England captains have had the grace to write to a displaced Test cricketer. But then, precious few captains have seen their front-line spinner dropped immediately after taking six wickets for seventy-nine runs in an Ashes Test!

After the traumas of the Tony Lock affair in the West Indies, I should have started to grow a second, thicker, skin. But with Lock now retired from English cricket and Fred Titmus recovering slowly from his accident, I fully expected to spend much of the summer of '68 taking on the likes of Bill Lawry, Ian Redpath, Doug Walters and Ian Chappell. In fact, it was quite impossible to decipher the workings of the selectors' minds that summer. For the First Test at Old Trafford, they named what was possibly the most brittle bowling attack England had ever sent into a Test match; John Snow, Ken Higgs and myself, supplemented by Basil d'Oliveira and Bob Barber. Bob was no more than a part-time bowler and he and Basil had taken only seven wickets between them at that stage of the season. We were therefore signalling our intention to play defensive cricket against a team which had made an unconfident start to its tour, and we paid the full penalty. In the first innings, I got some stick, none for seventy-seven off twenty-five overs. Lawry set his sights on me, I kept bowling length off-stump and he kept smearing me all over the place with the deliberate intention of knocking the youngster out of the firing line. But in the second innings, with the

Australians seeking to reinforce their enormous early advantage, I returned six for seventy-nine off thirty-three overs and my victims included the entire Australian middle order. Basil weighed in with 87 in the English second innings, and it was in this match that I learned a little more about the strangely convoluted personality of Geoffrey Boycott. One of the talking points of the Australian visit had been the inability of England's batsmen to 'pick' John Gleeson, the Australian spinner. He had been studied from all angles, a hundred theories had been expounded, but nobody could claim with complete certainty that they could spot his 'wrong un', the ball that turned sharply in a perverse direction. Basil had been studying the problem as hard as anybody, and suddenly he saw a solution. He called Boycott down the wicket and said: 'I've worked him out. This is what he does, he ...' Boycott interrupted the message. 'I know what he does,' he said. 'I've already worked him out. But don't go telling the others.' In later years, I would listen to Boycott's supporters deny that the great man's game was tainted by selfishness. And I would remember Old Trafford.

It was inevitable that heads would roll after England's 159-runs defeat, but after winning the individual awards for batting and bowling, Basil and I considered ourselves relatively secure. Nine days later, we were handed the photographs of the awards ceremony as we sat on the balcony and watched the Lord's Test, as 12th and 13th men. I never returned to the Test side that summer, Derek Underwood and, later, Ray Illingworth coming in to perform with considerable success. Basil returned only by default, the illness of Roger Prideaux bringing him in for the final, victorious Test at the Oval, where he scored his celebrated 158 with its equally celebrated repercussions. But for me, there was consolation. With the Fifth Test finished and the series drawn, I was playing for Surrey against Yorkshire up at Hull. I was wandering around the boundary boards down at long leg when a Yorkshire fan with a radio pressed to his ear shouted over to me: 'Pocock, you're in! You're in the tour side. Well done, lad.' I had made the team to tour South Africa, but the news which made all the front pages next day was the fact that Basil had been overlooked. Even after that brilliant 158, the Cape Coloured cricketer would not be returning to his native land as a member of the England party. I remember sitting in that dressing room at Hull and discussing the case with my Surrey colleagues. Micky Stewart, the captain, conducted an interesting exercise. He asked every member of the team to answer one question, on cricketing grounds alone: 'Would you have selected Basil d'Oliveira for the tour to South Africa?' All eleven players answered: Yes.

My own views about South Africa were then scarcely formed. I believed, and still believe, that the decision of the England selectors was made purely on merit, and that their subsequent decision to include Basil in place of the injured Tom Cartwright was also influenced only by cricketing considerations. In those days I held the comfortable, and wholly unrealistic view, that one could divorce sport from politics. But as I grew older and more mature, I came to see that the two cannot be slotted into separate compartments. This was partly through the experience of playing for Northern Transvaal in the winter of 1971-72. I greatly admired the way in which cricket had tried to put its own house in order and I felt desperately sorry for South African cricketers who would go to any lengths to get themselves accepted by the outside world. But I also realised that there was far more at stake than cricket. Britain has proved that you can only borrow a country, that, as with India and a host of other former possessions, you must eventually hand it back. If, by playing international cricket with South Africa, we even fractionally slowed down the process of handing the country back to the vast, oppressed majority, then we should not play with them. My evolving friendship with Basil was another important factor in my re-appraisal of the South African question. I remember imagining a situation whereby Diane would be flying into a South African city and I would be unable to meet her at the airport. My natural reaction would then be to ask Basil to pick her up in his car. Now, at that time, Diane would have been forced, by law, to sit in the back seat of that car. She could not sit in the front with Basil, since he was of a different race and colour. And that would have been unthinkable. Of course things have changed, and change is continuing, but until every hint and trace of apartheid is removed from that tragic country, I believe that we should not even contemplate sharing a cricket field with them. That may be a minority view among English cricketers, but it has become my deep conviction.

On the day after Basil's selection was announced, the South African Prime Minister, Mr John Vorster, declared that my friend was unacceptable as a member of the team. The MCC Committee, quite properly and promptly cancelled the tour. A trip to Pakistan and what was then Ceylon was hastily cobbled together and, it goes almost without saying, Basil's leg was unmercifully pulled throughout the new tour. As we dodged the riots in Lahore and Karachi and formed a desperate queue for the lavatory in Dacca, we would greet him with the same, tired quip: 'If it hadn't been for you, Basil d'Oliveira . . .'

*Basil d'Oliveira . . .
forever the young pro
with all the gleeful faults of youth*

Chapter eight

Come on Basil. If you get out now we can beat these white men

---

AT THE age of twenty-two the cricketer's career carries the hint of immortality. He lives in a world of endless summer, he thrives on the benefits of modest fame and, if he should ever stoop to such a calculation, he knows that his way of life is secure for the next twenty years. At such an age, two decades represents eternity. Then something happens to cast a small shadow; a serious injury, perhaps, or catastrophic loss of form . . . or the decline and demise of great players.

Ted Dexter and Kenny Barrington had played their last Test matches in the summer of '68. Different men of different styles and quite different characters, they shared a common genius for reducing a subtle and complex game to a thing of sublime simplicity. Now Tom Graveney was undertaking his final tour and a beautiful and significant era of English cricket was moving to its close. It was of Graveney that Sir Neville Cardus wrote: 'If some destructive process were to eliminate all we know about cricket, only Graveney surviving, we could reconstruct from him, from his way of batting and from the man himself, every outline of the game, every essential character and flavour which have contributed to cricket, the form of it and its soul, and its power to inspire a wide and sometimes great literature.' In the face of such an appreciation, mere praise is rendered redundant. Yet I was aware that the public grace and elegance of Tom Graveney was achieved at the cost of enormous mental stress, having watched him throughout the hazardous tour of the West Indies. He never sought to conceal his anxiety. He would put on his pads at the start of the innings, where normally a man going in at four would put on just his box and his thigh pad. Then, when a wicket fell, he would put on his gloves. The stand may have lasted for hours, but Tom would not remove those gloves, instead he would sit in the corner of the dressing room, declining to watch the cricket, just waiting and quietly worrying. By the time we reached Ceylon on that hastily arranged tour, he was no longer sure of his own ability. I remember a stranger asking him if he was nervous when he prepared to bat. I thought it an embarrassing question, but Tom took it seriously: 'Yes,' he said. 'At my age, at 41, you're always asking yourself the same question: Can you still do it? You know you've been a good player, but you know it has to end one day. Can you still do it? You can never rid yourself of that question.' Then, one afternoon in Colombo, Tom scored a superb hundred between lunch and tea. It was a wickedly hot day, around ninety-six degrees and with humidity of almost a hundred per cent, and Tom scored his runs off forty overs. 'Great knock, Tom' we said. 'Marvellous innings.' But Tom had no illusions. 'If I'm going to get a hundred these days, especially in heat like this, I've got to do it in a session,' he said. 'I know that when I walk out there. One session, that's all I can take.' He was out in the last over before tea. The weary old pro had paced himself perfectly.

Despite the intense heat, the best and most gentle memories of the tour could be traced to that short and soothing visit to Ceylon. The hospitality was courteous and the approach to cricket was civilised. It was not yet regarded as a matter of life and death, but simply as a game to be cherished and enjoyed. Certainly the breathtaking surroundings lent themselves to such an attitude. I recall playing the Central Province team at Kandy, perhaps the most spectacularly beautiful cricket ground on earth. John Murray was batting at lunch, and he came off the field and requested a pot of tea. In such a country, tea was scarcely an outlandish request, but after half an hour, Murray was still waiting for his beverage. He repeated the request at regular intervals, then he gave up in irritation and walked out to continue his innings. Ten minutes after the resumption of play, Murray's tea arrived, accompanied by two bearers in scarlet livery, white gloves and conical white hats. Naturally, we sent them out to Murray, who was in the process of chipping out a half-century. He reacted like a man who was accustomed to such treatment from the Middlesex ground staff; removing his batting gloves, sitting on the handle of his bat, lifting the cup from its silver tray and sipping tea with little finger impeccably cocked. The crowd did not know whether to giggle or applaud, so they did both. It was a serene little cameo, perhaps the last moment of serenity we were to experience on that turbulent tour.

After the tranquillity of Ceylon, we were unprepared for the chaos of Pakistan. We moved from crisis to crisis through a country torn between East and West, students and police, anarchy and order. Both the Pakistani politicians and the British diplomats cherished the interesting fallacy that the presence of an England team would somehow help to restore a kind of normality. In fact, the reverse was the case. Two of the three Tests offered the rioters a splendid stage for their protests, and they were not slow to accept the invitation. Only the Second Test, in Dacca, was played under reasonably tolerable conditions, and that was the game where the students made themselves personally responsible for crowd control. In addition to these minor distractions, we were facing a batting line-up which was pretty well implacable on its own wickets. You found yourself wincing as you glanced down the list of names; Mohammad Ilyas, Saeed Ahmed, Mushtaq Mohammad, Hanif Mohammad, down to Majid Jahangir, who was probably one of the ten best batsmen I ever bowled to in my life, coming in at seven and Intikhab Alam, shortly to take up a full-time place at Surrey, batting at nine. Only weariness and toil awaited English bowlers who hoped to run through that formidable assembly.

I was soon made aware that there were others, as yet unready for Test cricket, who promised to become equally accomplished. I was sharing a room with Roger Prideaux, the captain of Northants, who came back from an afternoon at the nets and fell on the bed in raptures of laughter. 'I have just signed a Pakistani fast bowler,' he said. 'Whoever comes to Pakistan and signs a fast bowler? I can't believe what I've done.' In fact, he had signed Sarfraz Nawaz on a contract which paid him the miserly sum of £400 for a season's trial. Prideaux had seen him bowl only in the nets and had taken the risk on the advice of Mushtaq. It was to prove a fascinating investment in a talented but sometimes controversial character.

I played in the First Test at Lahore. It was drawn, of course, as are most Tests in that part of the world and it was conducted in an atmosphere of bubbling unrest before a crowd permanently on the brink of riot. It was my fourth cap and I bowled unremarkably, with Intikhab's wicket my only reward. We then received a cable from the British High Commission in East Pakistan warning us not to come to that part of the country as our safety could not be guaranteed. When the news broke that we would not be travelling to Dacca, they promptly burned down the High Commission. This rather drastic action apparently provoked a few second thoughts, and twenty-four hours later, a further cable arrived assuring us that all was well. With the deepest misgivings we set off for Dacca, where the students promised us one organised demonstration each day and a Test match free from riots. They were as good as their word. I was left out of that game, in which Derek Underwood served as England's sole spinner, and at one stage, with England's first innings collapsing to 130 for seven, we were faced with the distinct possibility of defeat. It was d'Oliveira who negotiated us to safety with a massively patient and undefeated 114 which occupied four and three-quarter hours. He may have been unacceptable to South Africa, but he found himself strangely sought-after in Dacca. Mid-way through his long innings, Wasim Bari, the Pakistan wicket-keeper started to plead with him. 'Come on, Basil,' he said, 'if you get out now, we can beat these white men.' Basil stared at him. 'Don't start on me,' he said, 'I've had enough of that stuff.'

Colin Milburn arrived in Dacca shortly before the start of that drawn Test. He had been guesting in Western Australia and was flown in to cover for Colin Cowdrey's doubtful fitness. The entire team went to the airport to meet him as he lumbered, jet-lagged and exhausted, off the flight from Karachi. Immediately, we began to ply him with horror stories about primitive hotels, and his chins started to drop. In fact, we were staying in considerable comfort at the modern Inter-Continental Hotel in Dacca, but some of us retained memories of our first tour of Pakistan, and in particular we remembered the terrible place which brought us cockroaches with room service. We persuaded the coach driver to stop outside that infamous hotel. 'Here it is, Olly,' we said. 'Home.' The poor man almost broke down: 'We're not staying there. I can't stay there. I've not come all this way to stay at a gaff like that!' We ushered him in to register, and it was not until the tears started to glisten that we confessed the deception. Olly then went on to enjoy what was perhaps the most peculiar tour ever undertaken by a Test cricketer. He had a couple of nets in Dacca, then flew with the team to Karachi for the final Test. Olly was selected for that Test in place of Roger Prideaux. Colin Cowdrey won the toss and batted and Olly strolled out to the wicket in 105 degrees of heat and clattered the Pakistan attack for 139 runs. When he returned to the dressing room, his shirt was a wet rag. 'It's no good,' he said. 'I've got to go back to the hotel for a swim before I burst. Come on, Perce.' As twelfth man and with England batting, I wasn't needed at the ground, so we set off for the pool, splashed through the cool waters and listened to the match on the radio. And as we wallowed in that pool, we heard the rioting begin, heard the players being called from the field and, finally, learned that the tour was over. Olly had been in the country for ten days, he had batted in two net practices, scored a Test century and had never spent a moment in the field. Now he was going home.

In truth, few of us were displeased to be returning home. The discomforts were far less acute than I had known on my first tour,

CHAPTER EIGHT

yet in places they remained serious and distracting, and to these were added the constant tension, the threat of rioting and the occasional spells of genuine danger. And yet there were rewarding compensations. Playing in adverse conditions against gifted batsmen forced me to think more about my bowling, to revise my ideas and tighten my technique. Getting to know the Pakistani players and in particular, forming an enduring friendship with Intikhab represented another bonus. And then there were the ordinary Pakistanis, who loved their cricket and came to our matches in their tens of thousands. Whenever the service was poor or the food was dubious or the hotel room was less clean than we might have wished, I would remember the journey we made from Sahiwal to Lahore. On a bumpy road, sixty miles outside Lahore, Derek Underwood's bag containing all his kit bounced from the roof of our bus. A lorry driver spotted it by the side of the road, picked it up, drove to Lahore and tracked down the England hotel, where he handed in the bag. Now in that year of 1969, the whole of Underwood's kit would have fetched perhaps three times that lorry driver's annual salary. The thought never seemed to have crossed the man's mind. Underwood was not only a guest, he was a cricketer. What's more, he was a spinner. Honesty was therefore the only policy. Once again, I found myself reflecting that Pakistan not only suffered some appalling problems . . . it also enjoyed some admirable standards.

Chapter nine

Oh, well, perhaps I did get a touch

On Test match days at the Oval, they used to have a hospitality room which bore the notice: 'For the use of Surrey and Old England players only.' My county colleagues would take a sadistic delight in ushering me along to that room at close of play. 'Our Percy qualifies on both counts,' they would tell the man at the door. 'He plays for Surrey ... and he's the youngest Old England cricketer in the game.'

I would laugh, of course, and defend myself with all the cheap abuse at my command, but their jibe carried a sharp point. At the age of twenty-two, I had the vague suspicion that I should have to wait for many a long and frustrating year before resuming my Test career. Ray Illingworth had been named captain for the home series against West Indies and New Zealand in 1969, and he retained his post for the Tests against the Rest of the World which replaced the cancelled tour by South Africa in the following year. When the England captain is also the England off-spinner, every other off-spinner in the land must resign himself to the daily grind of county cricket and hope that one day somebody will remember his existence. I tried hard to put the situation into a sane perspective. The Surrey side was becoming a real force for the first time in years. I was enjoying my cricket and the laughter which was its constant companion. Perhaps success had come too quickly and a shade too easily to me, before I was in a position to savour it. I repeated all these things to myself until I almost believed them. Yet still I missed the Test scene, the challenge of competing with the very best players and the feeling that what I was doing was somehow important in a way that county cricket never could be. There were tours, of course.

CHAPTER NINE

For a first-class cricketer on the fringe of the England side, there are always tours. And if they lacked the bite and urgency of genuine Test match conflict, they were no less enjoyable for that. I made one such tour at the start of 1970, returning to Ceylon with an MCC team captained by Tony Lewis, then setting off on a huge, month-long sweep of the Far East.

It was a light-hearted, flag-waving expedition, made memorable by the personality of a great Yorkshireman. John Sydney Buller was the finest umpire I ever saw, and over the years I grew to love and admire that splendid band of men. Bowling for long spells and coming in off a short run, spinners get to know umpires. There were some whom you dreaded, a few you treated with contempt, but the vast majority were characters in their own right, and when you walked out in the morning, you greeted them like old friends. Arthur Jepson, the old Notts player, was one such official. A bluff, slightly crotchety individual, he would bridle at optimistic appeals. 'Owzat?,' he'd say. 'Are you kidding? Don't be a twat.' He would affect annoyance and refuse any further information. 'How many balls to come?', I asked him one day at the Oval. 'I'm not telling you,' he said. 'How many more?,' I repeated. 'Not saying,' he grunted. 'Right,' I said, 'I'm going all the way over to the square-leg umpire and I'm going to ask him the same question and when he tells me, you'll look an idiot.' Arthur thought about it, then he thrust out his hand, palm upwards, to reveal two pebbles. 'There you are,' he grunted. 'Three to come.' Cec Pepper was another who could reduce you to tears of laughter with a quick phrase. I remember playing Hampshire down at Bournemouth when Cec delivered a one-liner of such thunderous obscenity that I could not recognise the player at the other end through my heaving chuckles. When you consider that the Hampshire batsmen were Gordon Greenidge and Barry Richards, you will appreciate my predicament. On behalf of suffering cricketers everywhere, I was unreasonably delighted when Brian Taylor of Essex reported him to Lord's on the umpires' sheet for 'excessive farting'.

Wonderful men, yet Sydney Buller was the prince. The Australians believed him to be superhuman. If they played and missed and Syd gave them out caught behind, they'd walk back to the pavilion and say: 'Oh well, perhaps I did get a touch.' They could not believe that Buller might have made a mistake. I had known him as a quiet, serious official, sleeves rolled to the elbows and oozing efficiency. Until that tour of Ceylon, I never knew how deep ran his Yorkshire roots. We were coming home from dinner in Colombo one evening and Syd was walking a few yards in front of the main pack. Suddenly, this immensely dignified sixty-year-old

Syd Buller . . .
the umpire who was almost infallible

man broke into a jig of joy. When we reached him, he was standing outside a night-club called the Blue Leopard. 'Can you hear what they're singing in there?' he shouted. 'They're singing "Ilkley Moor," that's what they're singing. And we must be thousands of miles from Yorkshire. That's wonderful, that is.' Dear Syd. He had been doing a tremendous job on that tour, instructing umpires of lesser experience throughout the Far East, and on that night he was a truly happy man. Six months later he was dead, after collapsing during a match between Warwickshire and Nottinghamshire at Edgbaston. And the game had lost one of its most noble figures.

The other famous Yorkshireman on that Far Eastern tour was one Geoffrey Boycott. As ever, he had scored oceans of runs and, as ever, he had made the minimum concession to the social graces. I liked him for most of the time, although I found some aspects of his behaviour quite appalling. I wasn't able at the time to arrive at any firm assessment of his personality. He can be a very amusing character with an enormous knowledge of the game, yet I discovered that his colleagues only take him seriously when the topic is cricket. Then I found myself in his company on the twenty-six hour journey home from Hong Kong. Now in our capacity as official flagwavers, most of us had lived rather lavishly and were suffering from a fair amount of self-inflicted damage by the end of the tour. When I caught the flight at Hong Kong, I had not slept for the past two nights and I was feeling a trifle jaded. The feeling grew worse as the flight progressed and finally I visited the lavatory where I collapsed, crashing through the door and draping myself across the waiting Boycott. Suddenly, I heard that familiar voice barking a stream of orders: 'You! Sit him in that seat. You! Fetch the oxygen. You! Bring some cool, damp towels. Cool, mind. Not your luke-warm rubbish. You! Fetch him a cold drink.' Boycott was masterful, and I was vaguely aware that the cabin crew were moving faster than they had ever done in their lives. Geoffrey wasn't doing anything in particular, just putting the fear of God into everybody in uniform. It was an extraordinary exhibition of assertiveness and as I recovered through the flight, I was truly grateful. Geoffrey shrugged my thanks aside. 'Looked after you there, Perce, didn't I? You'd have been in some trouble if I hadn't been on this plane, eh?' For the next three or four seasons, he was to remind me of how he had looked after me on that plane from Hong Kong. Just in case the incident might have slipped my mind.

Almost two years passed before he showed me the other side of his nature once again. I was playing for Northern Transvaal in the Currie Cup and Geoffrey had been brought out by a wealthy sponsor to play for the same team. The sponsor had given Northern

Transvaal a list of games for which Boycott would be available, including the needle match against Mike Procter's Rhodesians. But Boycott had arrived slightly later than anticipated, and he felt he needed rather more than a week's preparation to face Procter. There was a colossal argument on the night before the match as Boycott forcefully stated his case, but eventually he was prevailed upon to play. Typically, he scored 107, grafting for his runs in his determination to show these people what the game was all about, and when his innings was over he sat in the dressing room and sipped a drink. The Transvaal captain was a charming man named Jackie Botten, who had been present at the pre-match argument but had played no part in the debate. As Boycott sat with his drink, Botten walked across to him, said 'Great knock, Boycs,' and held out his hand. Boycott just looked at him for a few moments, ignored the outstretched hand and turned away, leaving his captain feeling foolish and humiliated. I went over to Boycott five minutes later and said: 'What's going on? Why are you behaving like this?' And he shrugged. 'I've not come out here to be popular,' he said. 'I've just come out here to bat.' I told him a few home truths, not one of which made the faintest impression upon him. For the sake of a single handshake, he had created a new crop of enemies. The story would circulate and reinforce a host of preconceived opinions, and he didn't give a damn. He was only there for the batting.

But if I felt strongly about Boycott at that stage of my career, then I felt a good deal more strongly about his former county colleague. Like most cricketers, it was my abiding ambition to tour Australia with an England side. I had enjoyed a satisfying season with Surrey, I was a reasonably experienced tourist and a large section of the Press and pundits were supporting my cause. But when Ray Illingworth was once again named as captain, I knew that my chances were negligible. I sensed that Illy would not take me or, for that matter, any other off-spinner, because he would not want a player with whom he might be compared. The entire county circuit conceded his ability and respected him as a hard-bitten professional, but they knew of his shrewdness, his tendency to self-protection, his reluctance to submit himself to long spells of work and his habit of putting himself on to bowl at certain, favourable times of the day when mayhem was not in the batsman's mind. In this respect, he was utterly unlike his off-spinning contemporary Fred Titmus who, throughout his career, put his reputation and his average on the line and accepted the knocks along with the triumphs. Illy enjoyed the good days as well as anybody, but when the bad ones came along, he would all too often reach for an excuse.

My suspicions about the selection for Australia were miserably confirmed. Every other off-spinner in England was overlooked. Don Wilson of Yorkshire was given the vote as third spinner after Illingworth and Underwood and I suffered my most savage disappointment. Wilson was one of the warmest characters and most consistent players in county cricket, but his tour performance scarcely justified his selection. In the brutal words of Wisden: 'Wilson was completely out of his depth and took four of his six first-class wickets against Tasmanian batsmen.' But Illy could point to results as his justification, for England won the series, secured the Ashes and the captain returned home a hero. And if I had other, different opinions about his merits, then I was keeping them to myself.

*Geoffrey Boycott of the broad bat,
stern frown and uncompromising attitude.
With Boycott, the public face symbolises the private man.
His relentless devotion to the pursuit of runs and records
earned him respect,
but that curiously complex personality resisted popularity.*

Chapter ten

Will somebody tell me what is happening

THERE is a night club in Southampton where they serve a type of champagne so potent that Gordon Greenidge can bowl out a fine batting side just eight hours after they have supped it. The Surrey captain carried out a practical experiment one wild September night in 1971, as a result of which Greenidge returned figures of five for 49 with some of the most mediocre trundling ever seen in championship cricket. And nobody cared, not even Micky Stewart, who usually held the view that winning was the only good reason for playing cricket. In fact, Stewart cared least of all that day, for after nine years of sweat and toil, he had brought the county championship back to Surrey.

Typically, we had done our best to fumble the chance. In mid-August we were loitering in seventh place, then we put together five successive victories which left us needing fourteen points from the last two games to overtake Warwickshire. The champagne was produced in the penultimate match at the Oval, but Glamorgan's last-wicket pair held out and sent us down to Hampshire needing six points for victory. I helped to jeopardise our prospects by running out John Edrich and tossing away a fifth batting point. And then it rained, and we waited, cursed and did a good deal of praying. We needed to take four wickets to win two points in those days and Hampshire's first four batsmen — Greenidge, Barry Richards, David Turner and Roy Marshall — were depressingly formidable. But we chipped away; past Richards, past Greenidge, past Turner after an agonising wait, and then Intikhab flicked the edge of Richard Gilliat's bat, Arnold Long held the catch at the wicket and as I ran in from fine leg I knew that this was the most marvellous moment I would ever know in county cricket. Micky's wife, Sheila, ran on to embrace him. Stuart Surridge, then the Chairman of Cricket, strode on to the field to congratulate the entire side. A magnum of champagne was hauled out on to the ground and we stood and drank the first of many glasses as the Hampshire members greeted our achievement by roaring: 'Get on with the game!.'

Stewart had played in the Surrey side which won the title seven times in a row back in the fifties. He later said that he would have swapped all seven victories for that single success in 1971, and you could easily understand his reasoning. Things had been almost too easy in the halcyon days. With an attack of Bedser, Loader, Laker and Lock, nobody ever wondered whether the opposition could be bowled out; the only question was which bowlers would knock them over most swiftly on the helpful pitches of the day. Surridge had once declared, out of sheer boredom, when Surrey were in the eighties against Worcester. They then bowled them out for 25. But Stewart had built the '71 side slowly and from the rawest of material. Unlike the great side, he had won his championship despite being cursed by a low, slow lifeless Oval pitch: 'I've seen more movement in a graveyard,' said Cec Pepper. Only once in that year did Surrey take all twenty wickets to win a county match, an extraordinary statistic in a championship season, and of Geoff Arnold's 83 wickets in 1971, only twenty-four were taken at the Oval. So placid was that pitch that Arnold Long would stand just eleven yards back when keeping to Arnold at the Oval; on certain other pitches he would double the distance.

It was only in later years that I came to appreciate the true quality of Stewart's achievement, not simply in overcoming the problems of the pitch but in welding some diverse and difficult personalities into a powerful and cohesive team. The most interesting problems were posed by the Pakistani batsman Younis Ahmed who was, concidentally, the most important player in the side. Younis was a prolific scorer with the invaluable knack of playing his biggest innings when they were most urgently required. He also had the less attractive knack of infuriating just about everybody he played with or against, and not least the other major batsmen in the Surrey side. Neither John Edrich nor Graham Roope, who had frequently to bat with Younis, was happy with the arrogance of his attitude or the disdainful manner in which he treated the best efforts of his colleagues. Younis featured in several lucrative partnerships at the Oval in that season, yet very few were happy collaborations. He simply refused to make the customary allowances. If there is a mix-up over a short single and both batsmen escape by virtue of a wild throw, the normal form is to meet in the middle of the wicket and talk things through. Younis would have none of this. He would remain in his crease, throw an accusing glare at his partner and get on with his game. In later years he mellowed significantly and even became the willing and uncomplaining butt of much of the dressing room humour, yet he did not seek popularity. Like Geoffrey Boycott, he never thought it an ambition worth pursuing.

Younis would bring the worst out of players like Roope and Arnold, both of whom were easily persuaded that the whole world was in conspiracy against them, while Bob Willis was never really happy at Surrey since he was eternally uncertain of his first-team place. Willis was a classically raw fast bowler. He used to run in and bring the ball down as fast as he could from his tremendous height. When he started, he would either bowl short or bowl half-volleys; he couldn't be certain of hitting the wicket on a length. When he went to Warwickshire, in the season after Surrey's title victory, he started to find his length and became the great Test bowler that the world recognised. It was in Test cricket that he fulfilled his potential, since he was never strong enough to answer the demands of the seven-day county circuit.

With men such as these, as well as superb professionals like Robin Jackman and Stewart Storey and the lavishly gifted Intikhab, Micky Stewart put together his title team and developed the arts of man-management which were to serve English Test cricket so well in years to come. I enjoyed being a part of it, and most of all I enjoyed the personal spasms of success which came my way in that period.

The championship season brought me my first hat-trick, a slightly implausible affair on a big turner down at Guildford. Jim Yardley was the prospective victim, a left-hander who slashed everything through the gully. So celebrated was this shot of Yardley's that sides regularly posted three gullies for him, each standing within two yards of the next man. I bowled him a good delivery which pitched leg stump and turned a lot. He slashed at it and, even pitching leg stump, the open face of the bat sent it screeching into the gully, where the extraordinary reflexes of Roope knocked it up for Storey to complete a diving catch.

If the hat-trick was a shade unlikely, then the events at Eastbourne in the following season were really quite absurd. On a warm August evening, Surrey were being soundly beaten by Sussex. Set to score 205 for victory, Sussex were easing towards their target at 187 for one with three overs remaining. My own figures at that stage were wholly undistinguished; fourteen overs, one maiden, no wicket for 63 runs. It was one of those days when you just wanted to get the game over and put it down to unhappy experience. Then, at precisely six

*Micky Stewart . . .
the epitome of the English professional
— and the finest captain I ever played under*

CHAPTER TEN

o'clock, the telephone rang in the visitors' dressing room; Arthur McIntyre was calling from London to seek details of the defeat. 'They're just wrapping it up now,' he was told.'We've had it. Hallo, Percy's got a wicket.' Out of morbid curiosity, Arthur decided to hold the line for the last rites, and by the end of the over he was quite certain that he was the victim of an elaborate practical joke. With my first ball I bowled Geoffrey Greenidge. Mike Buss kept out the second ball, but I bowled him with the third. Jim Parks took two off the fourth, failed to score off the fifth and I caught and bowled him with the last ball of the over. Sussex were 189 for four wickets and required sixteen off the last two overs. Roger Prideaux and Mike Griffith took eleven runs off the next over, bowled by Robin Jackman, and when I began the final over of the match, they needed five runs to win. 'You still there, Coach?', said the man in the dressing room. 'I think Percy's got them worried.'

In years to come, I would look back and smile at that over, especially on those days when the wicket was dead, and the outfield like glass and the ball insisted on hitting the middle of the bat. With the first ball, I had Prideaux caught by Jackman. Mike Griffith, the Sussex captain came in on the hat-trick ball and was snapped up by Roy Lewis. Enter Jerry Morley for the third ball of the over. And exit Jerry Morley, stumped by Long. Four wickets in four balls, and still they needed five runs to win. 'What's happening? Will somebody tell me what is happening,' screamed the dressing room telephone, but nobody could break away from the cricket to relate the improbable story. John Spencer spoiled the sequence by scoring a single off the fourth ball of the over. Four to win off two balls, and with the first of those I bowled Tony Buss. The final delivery was addressed to Dulip Joshi, who swung strongly and hopefully, took a single and was run out going for the second. Sussex had finished on 202 for nine and the match was drawn.

The statisticians seized on the details like beggars at a banquet. Five wickets had fallen in that last over, a record for all first-class cricket. Sussex had lost eight wickets for fifteen runs in twenty minutes and eighteen balls. The final over had taken ten minutes to bowl, and at the end of it my analysis read: sixteen overs, one maiden, seven for sixty-seven. The spell included a hat-trick. four wickets in four balls, six wickets in nine balls (a world record), seven wickets in eleven balls (another world record) and five wickets in six balls (which equalled the world record). At last, the telephone was picked up. 'Coach,' they said. 'You're never going to believe this.'

But the days of real achievement at Surrey passed all too quickly. Stewart allowed himself to be persuaded to lead for one more season, which was a mistake. Having achieved his championship ambition in 1971, he lost a little of his old drive. The side relaxed and finished in a miserable twelfth position and Micky left the game on a far more sober note than any of us would have wished. He was replaced as skipper by John Edrich, an apparently logical appointment and, on the face of it, an immediately successful one, as we finished runners-up in John's first season as captain. But the players knew that the results were flattering. After the energy and full-hearted enthusiasm of Stewart, the Edrich approach offered a sad comparison. His interest in the team appeared no more than polite, and although he remained a genuinely great player, his leadership qualities were minimal. At the close of that season, the senior players went to the committee and told them we would support whoever the club chose to name as captain for the following season, but we added that we did not feel that Edrich should continue to captain the side. We stressed that we were speaking not from sour grapes but from a position of strength, having just finished second in the championship. The committee reacted in a manner more appropriate to the twenties than the early seventies and they said, in effect: 'Who the hell do these players think they are, telling us who they want to captain the side?' We realised, far too late, that our action had almost certainly secured Edrich the job.

We knew, quite obviously that a vote of no-confidence in the skipper would leave an unpleasant and lingering taste at the club. On a professional level, relations between captain and players had broken down to such a degree that we believed they were beyond repair. Edrich himself treated the affair seriously yet phlegmatically. 'You're wrong. I can do the job and I'll show you I can do it,' he said. Privately, he placed the blame for the whole episode on Stewart Storey who was, in reality, the least militant of the players. As one who had felt more strongly than most about things, I thought I had to let John know the true facts. We were travelling to an away match when I told him that I had played a far more active part than Storey in the brief rebellion, that I had nothing against him as a man and certainly nothing but admiration for his cricketing ability, but I believed that he was not awarding the job the total concentration it deserved. He seemed to accept my good faith and said he would try to change his approach. I knew he couldn't, but that's what he said. During his five years as captain of Surrey, our only honour was the Benson and Hedges Cup, which we won in 1974. It was welcome and it was duly celebrated, but it wasn't like winning the championship. And even as we sat in the Lord's dressing room and drank from the bubbling bottles, some of us remembered an endless evening in a Southampton night-club, when we drank champagne and toasted the future . . . and greeted the arrival of a false dawn.

County Championship Match
SUSSEX v. SURREY
at Eastbourne, August 12, 14, 15, 1972

Surrey

*M. J. Stewart not out	34	— not out	1
R. M. Lewis c Greenidge b M. A. Buss	72	— st Parks b Spencer	28
D. R. Owen-Thomas c Parks b Spencer	31	— c Griffith b M. A. Buss	32
Younis Ahmed c Parks b Phillipson	26	— c A. Buss b Joshi	26
G. R. J. Roope not out	43	— not out	21
M. J. Edwards c Joshi b M. A. Buss	81	— c Phillipson b Spencer	6
Intikhab Alam (did not bat)		— c Spencer b Joshi	6
B 6, l-b 7	13	B 4, l-b 6	10
(4 wkts., dec.)	300	(5 wkts., dec.)	130

A. R. Butcher, †A. Long, P. I. Pocock and R. D. Jackman did not bat.

Sussex

G. A. Greenidge c Long b Butcher	6	— b Pocock	68
P. J. Graves b Pocock	35	— c Roope b Jackman	14
R. M. Prideaux not out	106	— c Jackman b Pocock	97
M. A. Buss c Long b Pocock	8	— b Pocock	0
†J. M. Parks c Roope b Intikhab	29	— c and b Pocock	2
*M. G. Griffith not out	29	— c Lewis b Pocock	6
J. Spencer lbw b Intikhab	0	— not out	1
J. D. Morley (did not bat)		— st Long b Pocock	0
A. Buss (did not bat)		— b Pocock	0
U. C. Joshi (did not bat)		— run out	1
B 6, l-b 7	13	B 4, l-b 8, w 1	13
(5 wkts., dec.)	226	(9 wkts.)	202

C. P. Phillipson did not bat.

In a match shortened to little more than two days by rain three declarations brought the possibility of a result in the final overs of the day. In the event, the match was drawn but not before the remaining spectators had witnessed the most dramatic burst of wicket-taking in first-class cricket history.

Sussex, needing to score 205 for victory in 2¼ hours, were 187 for 1 with three overs of the compulsory twenty to be bowled. A second-wicket partnership of 160 in 107 minutes between G. A. Greenidge (68 n.o.) and R. M. Prideaux (92 n.o.) had made a Sussex victory apparently inevitable. Pocock's analysis at this stage was 14-1-63-0. Then, at exactly six o'clock, he started his fifteenth over.

Ball	Striker	Result	Total	Runs Required	Balls left
1	Greenidge	bowled	187-2	18	17
2	M. A. Buss	no run	187-2	18	16
3	M. A. Buss	bowled	187-3	18	15
4	Parks	two runs	189-3	16	14
5	Parks	no run	189-3	16	13
6	Parks	caught by bowler	189-4	16	12

Prideaux (4, 1) and Griffith (0, 0, 6, 0) took eleven runs off the next over bowled by Jackman and five runs were needed to win when Pocock began the final over . . .

Ball	Striker	Result	Total	Runs Required	Balls left
1	Prideaux	caught by Jackman	200-5	5	5
2 i	Griffith	caught by Lewis	200-6	5	4
3 ii, iv	Morley	stumped by Long	200-7	5	3
4	Spencer	one run	201-7	4	2
5 iii, v	A. Buss	bowled	201-8	4	1
6	Joshi	run out going for second run	202-9	3	—

Five wickets had fallen in the over — a record for all first-class cricket — and Sussex had lost eight wickets for 15 runs in twenty minutes (18 balls). The historic last over had taken ten minutes to bowl. At the end of it Pocock's analysis read 16-1-67-7.

THE STATISTICS

i. **Hat-trick** — Pocock's second in first-class matches.
ii. **Four wickets in consecutive balls** — the third instance by a Surrey bowler, the others being by:
    H. A. Peach v. Sussex 1924
    A. R. Gover v. Worcestershire 1935
iii. **Five wickets in six balls** — equalling **WORLD RECORD** held by:
    W. H. Copson: Derbyshire v. Warwickshire....................... 1937
    W. A. Henderson: N.E. Transvaal v. Orange Free State 1937-38
iv. **Six wickets in nine balls** — **WORLD RECORD** beating six in twelve by:
    P. G. H. Fender: Surrey v. Middlesex................................ 1927
    R. J. Crisp: Western Province v. Griqualand West 1931-32
v. **Seven wickets in eleven balls** — **WORLD RECORD** beating seven in fifteen by:
    H. Verity: Yorkshire v. Nottinghamshire 1932

Chapter eleven

Do me a favour, Perce.
Bring me back a Mars bar

PARTING had never been easy. However much we rehearsed the moment, the day of departure always came as a painful surprise. We had spoken about it many times over the years and Diane had admitted her dilemma; she wanted me to become a successful Test cricketer, with all the satisfaction, fame and modest fortune such status entailed, yet she knew that if I achieved my ambition, our separations would grow longer and more frequent. But we had made our decision and she was about to cope with the consequences. Now pregnant with our second child, she settled our small daughter into a push-chair and set off with young Sami for an hour's shopping in Reigate. A few minutes later, I picked up my bags, walked out into the late November afternoon and drove away on a four-month tour of India, Sri Lanka and Pakistan.

This time, she would not be coming out to join me, since Diane's pregnancy and Sami's age made the long and harrowing journey an impractical proposition. I had passed through all the stages which a cricketer who is also a family man will readily recognise; months of county bowling with the selectors in mind, days of indecision as they came to their conclusions, nights of celebration when I was named for the tour . . . then the realisation that I was leaving long before the worst of the winter, and would not return until Spring was into its stride. In those circumstances, the cricketer has a choice: he can spend the four months slouching around the sub-continent and cursing the absence of home cooking and home comforts, or he can immerse himself in the challenges of his game and the company of his colleagues. After an absence from Test cricket of almost four years, I was aching to prove that my game was still adequate, and I was blessed by some of the most diverting and appealing colleagues that MCC ever had the good sense to send abroad on its behalf. There really was no choice to be made.

I returned from my wildernesss years to discover profound changes in the England party. Only four other players remained from the side which had toured Pakistan in 1968-69, Keith Fletcher, Derek Underwood, Bob Cottam and Alan Knott. But Norman Gifford was there, and so was Jackie Birkenshaw, and between them they set the high-spirited, hard-working tone which characterised the expedition. Underwood and I were in the privileged position of being the Test match bowlers, leaving Gifford and Birkenshaw to play in the Zone games and provide the bulk of net bowling. It was a large and unglamorous undertaking, yet they set about it with enormous good humour. Indeed, I think I saw the smile leave Birkenshaw's face just once in the four months when he walked into his hotel room after a hard day's practice and saw a huge mosquito net draped across his bed. 'Nets!' he shouted. 'I spend the whole tour in the nets and now they're putting them up in me bedroom!' Gifford, who even then was one of the more experienced players in the squad, was equally selfless. He spent his trip chivvying, encouraging, scolding and organising, and he did them all to memorable effect. Gifford and Birkenshaw; hard, unyielding English professional cricketers. Once again I realised that the game holds no higher praise.

Tony Lewis was an interesting captain, a man who exuded charm, enjoyed all the social graces and appeared equally at home in dinner jacket or cricket sweater. He also possessed an excellent technique against spin bowling; where the pace of a vintage West Indian attack would certainly have overwhelmed him, the subtle spin of the Indians brought the best from his batting. If there were problems, then they were minor ones, and they sprang from the absolute authority he was accustomed to wielding in his own county of Glamorgan. Lewis knew his own mind and issued decisive instructions. It could not be said of him, as it was said of Robin Marlar during his days as captain of Sussex, that: 'His players followed him on to the field out of a sense of curiosity.' But he was a shade dictatorial and I had a passing brush with him early in the tour when he repeatedly over-ruled my field placings. We exchanged a few words at the time, and at close of play I asked to have dinner with him. I thought very hard about the best way to formulate my complaint. What I really wanted to say was: 'I have spent more time thinking about my off-spin bowling in one month than you have in your whole career. I'm not some lackey playing for Glamorgan on a sandy beach down in Swansea. When I set a field, it's for a specific

CHAPTER ELEVEN

reason. It's not because I don't know where else to put them.' But the years had brought a tiny degree of tact. I told him that Micky Stewart was the best captain I had ever played under and he overruled me twice in the average season. Lewis had already overtaken Stewart and the tour was scarcely under way. There was a real difference between bowling as a flight bowler on flat wickets in India and firing the ball in on great dusty turners down in Wales. He seemed a little surprised at this demonstration of independence, but he took my point and we got along amiably and productively for the rest of the tour. In fact, Lewis did such a good job of rallying the players at critical stages of the tour that it was generally agreed by both the Press and the team that despite the ultimate result it was the happiest tour they had known.

We were frequently grateful for his social expertise during that tour, with its ceaseless round of receptions and small-talk cocktail parties. Until you tour India, you have no conception of the extraordinary attention which is lavished upon an England touring team. Large crowds swarm around the English players in the streets, Indian newspapers are full of the tourists' most mundane activities and the most effective way of moving up the social scale is to secure their presence at a party. At the start of every week the manager, Donald Carr, would provide us with a list of forthcoming functions and the clothes we were expected to wear for them: the British High Commission — jackets, collars and ties; local cricket society — smart casuals; Indian Board of Control reception — jackets collars and ties. We would groan when the list was issued. 'What will we do at the Gymkhana Club?', we'd say. 'There'll be nobody there under ninety.' Then we would realise that there was nowhere else to go, that we might bump into somebody who was a bit different and, anyway, they would almost certainly give us a drink to pass the time. Then Lewis would charm them with a few words and we'd all troop back to the hotel and agree that it hadn't been so painful after all.

When it came to the Tests, we had the shrewd suspicion that the Indians might place a degree of faith in their spinners. In Bishen Bedi, they could offer a man who was probably the greatest flight bowler the game had ever known. I remember reading an appreciation of his art in which the writer said that he would go to a Test match 'just to watch Bishen Bedi thinking about his bowling,' and I completely understood those sentiments. His repertoire was enthralling. In a single over he would bowl from wide of the crease, up tight to the wicket, a gentle swinger then a slightly quicker ball; and all effected with those imperceptible variations of spin and speed which carried the gentle guarantee of deception. To these

*Bishen Bedi . . .
probably the greatest flight bowler the game has known*

mesmerising arts, he brought the attitude of a thoroughly decent man and an honest competitor. On occasion, a batsman would hurry down the pitch and drive him for four or six. And Bedi would applaud the stroke. Sometimes a colleague would chastise him for his generosity, but Bishen would never accept such criticism. 'If you can't enjoy this game,' he would say, 'what can you enjoy?' When Bishen Bedi played cricket, everybody enjoyed themselves. I still see him from time to time as he coaches the new generation of cricketers. His waist-line has advanced with the years, but he still moves with the fluency of a poem. The bounce, the swing and the masterful control of flight are all intact. 'Just turning the arm over, Percy,' he says. 'I can't really do it any more.' And he knows he is not telling the truth.

On that tour, however, even Bedi was outshone by the amazing Chandrasekhar, who revealed himself as the most dangerous bowler in the world on flat and lifeless wickets. I used to watch Chandra bowl his confection of leg-breaks, googlies and top-spinners as a batsman might watch Gary Sobers organise an innings. One day in Calcutta, he bowled for three hours at players like Mike Denness, Lewis, Keith Fletcher and Tony Greig with just three men on the off-side: mid-off, silly point at catching, and a slip. It was the only time I have ever seen batsmen of that quality struggle so desperately to score on a flat wicket. Incidentally, our shrewd suspicions about their faith in spin were amply justified. In the five-Test series, Chandra and Bedi bowled 663 overs between them and took sixty wickets. The most successful seam bowler was Abid Ali, who took three wickets and was listed in the averages as: 'Also bowled'.

My enforced break from Test cricket had sharpened my appetite to a degree which surprised me. I was desperately anxious to be involved. As we drove to the ground in New Dehli on the morning of the First Test, I remember saying to Lewis: 'I'm more wound up and excited at the thought of playing in this Test than any other Test I've ever played.' The captain just grunted. He had more things on his mind than the nervous chatter of his off-spinner. It was a dull and misty morning, difficult conditions for fielding, and I had dropped everything in the pre-match catching practice. India won the toss and batted, and as I walked down to fine leg at the early hour of ten o'clock, I clearly remember looking up into that sullen grey sky and praying: 'Please don't let anything come my way until this mist lifts.' It was not an effective prayer. With the second ball of the match, Geoff Arnold bowled a bouncer at the tiny Ramnath Parkar, who swung a savage hook and sent the ball spiralling into the mist in the general direction of fine leg. I squinted into the murky sky, took off at the gallop and wrapped my hands around the chance. From that point on, everything seemed to go right in the match. Although Chandra returned eight for 79 in our first innings, we played assured, convincing cricket and on the final day, Christmas Day, Lewis scored seventy undefeated runs to see us home by six wickets. Champagne in Dehli was a trifle thin on the ground, but somehow fifty bottles managed to find their way into our dressing room, where they were consumed in short order by both the team and the quorum of English fans. My memories of the evening are necessarily hazy, but I recall travelling back to the hotel in a bus driven by an exceedingly poor loser. The players had decided to throw the kit-bags inside the bus and make the ride on the roof to celebrate the victory, and the unhappy driver screeched from side to side of the road, searching out overhanging branches which might sweep away these insufferable Englishmen. It was hard to be away from home at Christmas, but that day had delivered memorable compensation.

Even when our luck started to turn, as it did in the next Test in Calcutta, the glow of that victory somehow seemed to warm the entire tour. We lost the Second Test by twenty-eight miserable runs, Chandra and Bedi picking up sixteen wickets between them, and this time the compensation came with the unrivalled thrill of playing in front of 75,000 spectators perched in the open stands, each of them clutching a radio which blared out a ball-by-ball description of the Test match. From the middle of Eden Gardens, we could hear every comment, every opinion; sometimes you laughed and sometimes you wanted to involve the pundits in furious argument. The hardest thing was to turn a deaf ear.

It was soon after this that we received death threats, allegedly from the Black September group. The English players, they said, would be picked off one by one; in alphabetical order, of all things. We were naturally worried, Dennis Amiss most of all, yet even so we were unprepared for the stringent reaction of the Indian authorities. Every man in the party was given an armed guard for the rest of the tour. He slept outside your room in the hotel corridor, when you walked out on to the field he walked the first fifteen yards with you, if you went to a party he sat by the door, watching, and when you visited a restaurant he occupied the next table. We once went to the cinema in Jamshedpur to watch Richard Burton in 'Raid on Rommel'. Seventeen players occupied the front row ... and in the row behind sat seventeen detectives. For a while, their constant presence was disconcerting, the sight of large men with machine guns patrolling outside your bedroom door was not as reassuring as the authorities intended. But we grew used to the situation and began to exploit it. The great thing about having a permanent police escort was that you always had a car at your disposal. Nobody was allowed to take a taxi, we travelled exclusively by jeep. One evening, we turned up at a party in our usual squadron of jeeps and our host's face fell as he opened the door. 'This is a dry State, we're not allowed to drink,' he said. 'If the police come in here, it's going to be a miserable party.' I went to work on my guardian angel. 'I'm afraid you can't come in,' I said. 'Private party, you see.' He insisted that he had to come in, that he could not let me out of his sight. 'All right, then,' I said. 'You can only come in if you drink this.' And I gave him a very weak Scotch which he knocked back in a gulp. The other players immediately plied their escorts with similar drinks, and the doors were thrown open. The Indian police had just swallowed their powers of arrest.

While we learned to make light of the situation, back home they were genuinely worried. I realised the extent of their concern when I sent Diane a present of an ornamental box from Madras. The shop posted the order from its central stores in Bombay, and when Diane received it she checked the date and postmark and realised that the team had yet to reach Bombay. She rang the police, who advised her to leave it at the end of the garden until the bomb squad arrived. They turned up in force and whisked it off to an open site in Oxted where they unwrapped the parcel with meticulous care, flicked open the small golden catch — and discovered an affectionate note from a thoughtful husband. Diane was eventually handed her present from the boot of a police car.

I was to meet Diane soon after that disturbing incident, and in circumstances which every tourist dreads. The Third Test was over and while I had returned the immensely satisfying match figures of eight for 142, England had lost by four wickets and fallen behind in the series. We had moved on to Jamshedpur when I received a cable from my brother asking me to call home immediately. Instinctively I sensed that something had happened to my father, who had been unwell for some time, but when I tried to telephone, I was told that there was a four-hour delay on calls to England. In desperation I dashed around to the house of a man named Rusi Modi, the chairman of one of the biggest companies in India, who was entertaining Tony Lewis to lunch by the pool. I explained my predicament and Mr Modi picked up the poolside telephone. 'I want a call to this number in England, and I want it within sixty seconds,' he ordered. The phone rang thirty seconds later, and I learned that my father was dead.

It was an appalling blow. He was a good and kindly man who had given me nothing but encouragement and sound advice, and one of the great joys of my career was the sight of my parents sitting in the

*Kandy, Sri Lanka . . .
remote, stunning, simply perfect.
Perhaps the most beautiful cricket ground in the world*

*Karachi, Pakistan . . . intense heat allied to fierce competition
make it one of the world's most challenging battlefields
for English Test cricketers*

pavilion and following my progress at the Oval and at cricket grounds all around the Home Counties. Donald Carr agreed that I should return home immediately, and as I left the hotel I met Peter Laker, who was covering the tour for the Daily Mirror. He offered a few words of condolence, then he made a request which every visitor to India will understand. 'Do me a favour, Perce,' he said. 'Bring me back a Mars bar.' Diane was waiting for me at Heathrow, but even as I greeted her, I was searching for my daughter. 'Why didn't you bring Sami?', I said. 'You told me she'd be here.' I was looking for the infant who rode in a push-chair or sat in her mother's arms. Diane pointed to a small girl, sprinting between the porters' trolleys. I had been away for barely ten weeks, but Sami was no longer a baby. Touring has its pleasures, but it also carries some heavy penalties.

When I returned to India, the team had drawn the Fourth Test. A small group of players, alerted by Peter Laker, met me at the hotel door. There were a few handshakes, a sudden scramble, and three dozen Mars bars disappeared before I reached my room. Despite the defeats, morale was high and remained so even after the drawn Fifth Test in Bombay which gave the Indians the series. The matches had been played in civilised fashion between sides who enjoyed mutual respect, and Englishmen who had lived in India for many years told us that we were the most popular team ever to visit the country. Certainly the Bombay public seemed to think so, for 50,000 spectators remained in the ground for an hour after the finish and demanded a lap of honour from the entire English party.

After a brief and idyllic visit to Sri Lanka, we travelled to Pakistan for three Tests, all predictably drawn, and crowd conduct followed its traditional pattern with a vigorous riot in Karachi. My fondest memories were of the Hyderabad Test, as I took five of the nine Pakistani wickets to fall and collaborated with Derek Underwood in a tenth-wicket stand of 55 which was a record for England v Pakistan Internationals.

Despite all the trials and despite my own personal tragedy, it had been a magnificent tour, one which held solid promise for the future of the English game. Keith Fletcher had been sent out to seize what the selectors publicly described as his 'last chance' to make the grade in Test cricket, and he had responded with a flood of runs. Chris Old revealed every sign of becoming a truly effective fast bowler. And then there was Tony Greig; extrovert and tactless, with an arrogance which was exceeded only by the scope of his talent. I remember feeling reasonably sure that we were going to hear much more from that young man.

Chapter twelve

Come on, Greigy, I think you'd better let me drive you home

THE stones came first, rattling like rifle shots against the dressing room walls, and they were followed by the heavy thump of bricks. Then came the crash of broken glass, the angry chanting and stamping and eventually, the moan of police sirens. I recognised each familiar noise. I could have recited their sequence. They were the sounds of an England cricket tour.

I sat in a corner of that dressing room in Trinidad, swearing softly and waiting for the arrival of the next brick. My latest come-back to Test cricket was precisely two days old, and as the chanting grew louder, the chances of it enduring into Day Three were looking distinctly slim. Keith Fletcher sat in the opposite corner, repeating the same phrase over and over again. 'It had to be Greigy, didn't it?,' he said. 'It just had to be Greigy.' He was right, of course. In February of 1974, there were those who believed Tony Greig to be the man most likely to start World War Three; a small riot in Port of Spain was scarcely a strain on his resources. A few minutes earlier, Bernard Julien had played the last ball of the day to Greig at silly point. Alvin Kallicharran, at the bowler's end, assumed that the day's cricket was over and started to stroll towards the pavilion, whereupon Greig hurled down his stumps from twenty yards and bellowed an appeal which the umpire accepted. Kallicharran had been run out for 142, and the population of Port of Spain was extremely angry. None, it must be said, was more angry than Kallicharran, and the sight of him breaking his bat in two upon the pavilion steps was the signal for the stones to fly. Greig appeared genuinely bewildered by all the fuss. The laws of the game had been observed, the umpire had ruled in his favour and, what the hell, that was the way you played the game, wasn't it? Certainly it was the way he played the game, because his South African upbringing had told him that it was the only way.

As I sat in the besieged dressing room, the memories of my own brief South African experience came crowding back. In particular, I remembered the activities of one resourceful wicket-keeper in a Currie Cup match who carried a competitive game to its limits. I was batting when drinks came out and the players gathered in small groups. The keeper wandered up to the wicket, nudged leg-stump half an inch closer to middle-stump and flicked off the exposed bail with the top of his pad so that it dropped behind the wicket. 'What do you think you're doing?,' I said, and he answered without a trace of shame. 'I'm practising,' he said. 'Our spin bowler bowls one down the leg side, the batsman sweeps and I flick off the bail and appeal. Hit wicket, see?' That was the way you played. I recalled, too, the story they loved to tell of Tiger Lance when he played in South Africa's final series against Australia in 1970. Ian Chappell cut a short ball, fell backwards and heard an appeal for a catch in the gully. 'Did you catch it,' he asked. 'Yes,' said Lance, and Chappell accepted his word and walked off. When he reached the dressing room, the furious Australians informed him that the ball had been taken on the half-volley. That evening, at a reception for both sides, Chappell sought out Lance and gave him a selection of his choicest phrases. Lance could not understand his attitude. 'You asked me if I caught it,' he said. 'You didn't ask if it bounced first.' The way you played . . .

Now Tony Greig was not a cheat, but he looked at the laws of the game, any game, with a lawyer's eye. He once played a celebrated golf match at the Wanderers course in Johannesburg with the Pollock brothers, Graeme and Peter, and Eddie Barlow. The stakes were high, the gallery was huge and when they reached the eighteenth green, the game rested on the putting ability of Greig and Peter Pollock. Confronted by a sixteen-footer, Pollock knocked it nervelessly into the hole, leaving Greig to sink a twelve-foot putt for a half. Greig stalked the putt from all sides, then he noticed Pollock's caddy holding the flag. 'It'll help my line,' he said, 'if you attend the pin.' As the caddy placed the pin in the hole, Greig crashed the ball against the caddy's foot and fell on his back, roaring with laughter. 'My ball struck your caddy. I claim the hole and we've won the match,' he yelled. And the crowd awarded him the applause of a hero. He was right, the rules of that time allowed it and one is permitted to take advantage of the rules.

With all these things in mind, I understood perfectly Greig's instinctive reaction at seeing Kallicharran leave his crease. You could

Tony Greig . . .
one of the most charismatic cricketers of his age

count on one hand the number of English professionals who would have taken similar action to Greig. Douglas Jardine would have done it forty years earlier without a quiver of conscience, Tony Lock could well have contemplated it while Wilf Wooller, down at Glamorgan, might have thought it an excellent idea. Of the English team in the West Indies in 1974, only Greig would have thrown down those stumps, and now we were coping with the consequences. By this time, the Trinidad crowd had seized on the political implications of the incident. 'Send the South African home,' they chanted.

Gary Sobers, with the style and the sensitivity which were his hallmark, saved the immediate situation by walking into our dressing room and saying: 'Come on, Greigy. I think you'd better let me drive you home.' The presence of Sobers was worth more than an army of escorts in the Caribbean, and with their chief target removed, the spectators' anger started to dissolve. They were finally placated completely when, after a two-hour meeting with the English management, the West Indies Cricket Board issued a statement saying that 'in the interests of cricket generally and of this tour in particular,' the appeal had been withdrawn and Kallicharran would resume his innings next morning. A lot of the English players resented the climb-down by our management. Although they could not approve of Greig's action, the umpire had upheld it and the laws had not been infringed. And if that decision should provoke the kind of riots which would lead to the cancellation of the tour, then so be it. Personally, I was too distressed even to contemplate cancellation. I had returned from the Indian tour as the leading wicket-taker and had been promptly overlooked for all the home Tests against New Zealand and West Indies. I was desperate for the chance to prove myself again, and privately I was enormously relieved when the concession was made. Next day there was a dreadfully artificial gesture of contrition when Greig, as arranged, walked to the centre of the pitch and offered Kallicharran an ostentatious handshake. The crisis had passed, but Greig had installed himself as the central character of the series. It was a role which he gladly accepted.

Even today, when I meet the survivors of that West Indies campaign, we speak of 'Greigy's tour,' since that is how we came to regard it. Mike Denness may have been the England captain, but as vice-captain Greig was by far the stronger character and it was he who set the tone and the temper of the tour. With obvious reservations, I actually liked the man. His style was to lead from the front with absolute commitment and when he asked you to bowl in a certain way or field in an exposed position, he received the response that his own example deserved. With Greig, the ends always justified the means, and it was on that tour that the dubious art of 'sledging'—verbally intimidating and provoking opposing batsmen—reached its most critical proportions. Greig believed that certain West Indies batsmen, notably Rohan Kanhai and Kallicharran, could be cajoled into playing an angry shot by an orchestrated campaign of abuse. The Australians had invented the concept, but Greig and the England close fielders now embraced it. We had an arrangement with the West Indians that each evening at close of play, the fielding side would entertain the batting side to drinks in the dressing room. In fact, it gave everybody a licence to sledge because they knew that the row would be patched up over a couple of beers in the evening. Things have improved enormously since those cynical days, but it took the excesses of Tony Greig to make people aware of the dangers. I spent a great deal of time in his company and enjoyed it immensely. He was an excellent colleague, a hard-working professional and he projected a fine public image, albeit outside the West Indies.

For all his hell-raising, both on and off the field, Greig eventually found time to come-of-age as an outstanding Test all-rounder, which was a considerable achievement against a West Indies side which had shed some of its old stars and was emerging as a new and fearsome force. The batting line-up was of a quality to make an ambitious spinner consider early retirement. Imagine finding a way past Roy Fredericks, Lawrence Rowe, Kallicharran, Clive Lloyd, Kanhai, Sobers, Deryck Murray and Julien, only to find Keith Boyce striding down the pavilion steps as a positively homicidal Number Nine! It was unquestionably the most talented assembly I had ever bowled at, and in that First Test they simply flexed their muscles in scoring 392. It was during that first West Indies innings that my doubts concerning the captaincy of Denness took shape. I had been bowling pretty well in a long spell, taking the odd wicket and conceding around two and a half runs per over, when Boyce came in and began to play his shots at the other end. When he came down to my end, he hit the first ball for six. They were still cheering that stroke when he dropped to one knee and swept me first-bounce into the crowd for four. I was preparing to bowl the third ball when Mike Denness walked the length of the pitch and took my arm. 'I'm talking to you just for appearances,' he said. I was bewildered. Had he come across with a firm instruction or a change of field, I could have accepted it, but this was pure public relations; the captain was telling the world that he was in charge. 'You're making me look a bit daft,' I said, but he shook his head. 'Just appearances, Percy,' he said and he walked back to his position. Now I knew that Boyce never left his crease, that he played all his shots from that crease, so I

CHAPTER TWELVE

tried him with a yorker. For the first time in my experience, he came dancing down the wicket and met it on the full, struck it like a shell and holed out to Geoffrey Boycott at extra cover. If I was delighted, then Denness was ecstatic. In the eye of the public, a few words from the captain had worked the trick. Appearances had been maintained.

But our delight was short-lived. Although I took five wickets for 100, the West Indies came through to a seven-wicket victory, England had lost her first Test match in the Caribbean for twenty years and the outlook for the rest of the series was entirely ominous.

I did not take a wicket in the next Test and I conceded 152 runs, yet I shall forever regard it as the finest and most professional bowling performance of my career. It was my thirteenth Test match and it had taken me far too long to learn how to bowl. All but one of those Tests had been played outside England, on flat, unhelpful wickets which demanded pragmatic, economical bowling. I had tried to meet those requirements, but without much conviction, since I preferred to experiment with flight and changes of pace. Now, at last, I realised the value to the side of disciplined, defensive bowling. I could not expect sensational results. If I bowled a maiden over to these batsmen, I would deserve a round of drinks, and a couple of wickets would represent an outrageous bonus. So I set out to pin them down, and the figures still give a warm glow: fifty-seven overs, fourteen maidens, none for 152. It was the turning point in my development as a spin bowler.

Tony Greig shared my view that the Kingston pitch was probably the flattest in the history of Test cricket, but he was also impressed by my success in keeping these superb players relatively quiet on a ground with only a fifty yard boundary. With typical boldness, he decided to try his arm at off-spinning for the first time in a first-class match. He looked at the line-up of left-handers—Fredericks, Sobers, Lloyd and Kallicharran—and decided that off-spin was the only way to contain them. He set himself a 7-2 off-side field, square third man, deep extra cover and long-off, three 'sweepers' on the boundary and a slip. It was less than romantic, but it did have the effect of applying the brakes and reducing the amount of time which the English batsmen would need to survive and save the match. I remember Donald Carr coming into the dressing room at the end of one session and saying in true-Brit fashion: 'Greigy, I'm not terribly sure I like your field.' Greig's reply, perhaps fortunately, has slipped my mind. The West Indies duly posted their massive score, 583 for nine declared, but they paid for their earlier tardiness. Dennis Amiss played an innings of sound technique and implacable character for an undefeated 262, the tailenders managed to stay with

*Sir Gary Sobers . . .
to have shared his company was a pleasure
and to have played in his generation was a privilege*

CHAPTER TWELVE

him for lengthy periods—including P.I. Pocock, who plundered four runs in eighty-five minutes—and England survived to earn an improbable draw.

By now, Greig had developed a taste for off-spin, 'I like this spinning lark, Perce,' he used to say. 'It's comfortable, and your shirt's not wringing wet when you come off the field.' He flaunted his new affection with six for 164 in the Third Test in Barbados. But by now the West Indies were batting in a manner which exceeded even their own lofty reputations, and it was Rowe's turn to inflict the most savage punishment with a breathtaking triple-century. There were others in that team who were held in greater awe, but Rowe was possibly the most compact player I ever saw. Trying to get him out was like trying to open a can of beans with a feather, in the end you just bowled and hoped. And he gave you very slim grounds for hope. But we escaped once again, largely through Greig's innings of 148, and the team clung to the conviction that while he was in this sort of form, anything was possible. I missed the Fourth Test in Guyana with a split finger, the eternal curse of the off-spin bowler, and while the match was largely ruined by rain, we managed to put some pressure on the West Indies for the first time in the series, largely and inevitably through Greig, who contributed another century.

In fairness, we should have been dead and deeply buried long before that Fifth and final Test in Trinidad, for the West Indies were laying the foundations of a cricket team which was destined to dominate the world game for the next decade. The quality of their batting spoke for itself, Lance Gibbs was still bowling masterly off-spin and if they could not offer opening bowlers of truly terrifying pace, then Boyce and Julien were sufficiently lively to demand wary respect and the introduction of Andy Roberts gave a hint of real speed to come.

The English effort, moreover, had been streaked by individual disappointment. The three pace bowlers, Bob Willis, Chris Old and Geoff Arnold, took just twelve wickets between them in the series. Mike Denness proved himself something of a disappointment as a Test batsman, and saddest of all, young Frank Hayes from Lancashire endured a miserable tour and scored just sixty runs in seven innings. He had introduced himself to Test cricket with a century against the West Indies at the Oval a few months earlier, and I honestly believed that he had more natural attributes than any other English batsman I have ever seen. He had a tremendous eye and enormous physical strength, he got on to shots quickly, struck the ball with savage power and he was as fast in the field as Clive Lloyd. I cannot think of another English player who looked more completely equipped to become one of the legends of the game, yet he was unable to handle the pressure of Test cricket, and it was that one flaw in his temperament which cost him the career his talent demanded. With all this, he was an extremely entertaining man. He enjoyed a drink, enjoyed it so much that we called him 'Fish.' The management recognised this tendency and banned him from rooming with Mike Hendrick, since they thought they were such a bad influence on each other. Frank Hayes never really recovered from that protracted disaster in the Caribbean, and Test cricket was deprived of a major and original talent.

And then there was Boycott, the mystery wrapped in an enigma. In that year of '74 he should have been at the very peak of his powers, and with the series offering him the chance to measure himself against some of the finest batsmen in Test history, we expected a torrent of runs. Somehow, it never happened; the torrent shrunk to a thin stream, and although he contributed innings of 99 and 112 to that final Test, he was never the grimly commanding figure we had known. He would doubtless present a hundred reasons for this comparative decline, he would also point out that he finished with an average of 46 for the series, but he was rarely happy and I believe the truth lay in his sudden vulnerability against fast bowling. Tony Greig was later to write that Boycott had a tremendous ability to be where fast bowlers were not. I think that was grossly unfair; Boycott was never afraid of pace, indeed, I don't think he knew a moment's physical fear on a cricket pitch. But he certainly went through a stage where he just couldn't handle it from a technical point of view. He used to freeze and tuck himself into extraordinary positions, and time and again he would be hit by balls he should have dismissed. I am certain that it was the most testing time of his career. He always played with one eye on posterity, he had made himself into a great player and he knew that history would judge him by his ability to remain at that peak. Great players do not come and go, theirs is a talent which endures for a decade or more. This vulnerability against pace might cost him his place in history, and he was seriously concerned. For the first time in his life, he was tormented by self-doubt; never a gregarious man, he disappeared into his shell as he attempted to work things out. It was significant, yet scarcely surprising, that half a year later Boycott was to withdraw from the tour to Australia and the conflict with Lillee and Thomson: 'because I wouldn't be able to do myself justice.'

But if there were disappointments, there were also successes and they lay principally in the inspired form of Amiss, who averaged 82 for the series, the performances with bat and gloves of Alan Knott, whose excellence we were already taking for granted, and. of course,

CHAPTER TWELVE

the extraordinary achievements of Greig. He saved the best until last, that memorable Fifth Test which England had to win to salvage the series. England had batted first and, despite Boycott's grafting had managed an inadequate total of 267. The wicket was turning slightly at one end, and it was from that end that I took the first couple of wickets, Fredericks and Kallicharran. But West Indies prospered steadily and had reached 224 for three wickets, when Greig began to enjoy success from the turning end, sweeping up the remaining eight wickets and returning figures of eight for 86. Boycott then quarried a century in six and three-quarter hours, and West Indies were set 226 to win. Once again it was off-spin, Greig's off-spin, which overcame their ambitions. England won by 26 runs with an hour to spare and Greig finished with five for 70 to give himself thirteen wickets in the match, twenty-four in the series. He was never again to produce the devastating spin bowling which he discovered in that Test match, but never again did it matter so much. On that April evening in Port of Spain, the world seemed to lie at his feet. He was vice-captain of England, a prolific and exciting batsman, a brilliant close catcher, an excellent seam bowler and now, we learned, a spinner good enough to devastate the strongest batting side in the game. There were many that evening who were ready to acknowledge him as the complete cricketer, the most gifted all-round player on the planet.

But they were wrong. That title belonged to the slim, self-effacing gentleman, who had walked quietly away from the ground, leaving the night to the celebrating Englishmen. Typically, he told nobody of the decision which was forming in his mind. Gary Sobers had played his last Test match, but he was never a man to ruin a party.

Chapter thirteen

Don't even try to get him out

THE Queen was polite and charming, but I sensed that cricket was not her consuming interest. I met her during the Lord's Test of 1976. While the English batsmen were fending off the likes of Michael Holding and Andy Roberts out in the middle, Brian Close sat in the pavilion and chatted with the Duke of Edinburgh and I engaged in twenty minutes of small talk with Her Majesty. She was amazed by the advertising boards around the ground and the new air of commercialism in the game. She felt sorry for mothers who had to play cricket with their children and risk injury from that hard and dangerous ball. Then I looked across that huge ground with its capacity crowd and its enormous contingent of West Indian fans; dancing, singing, rattling cans and generally living out every moment of the match with Clive Lloyd's team. 'Have you ever watched a match in the West Indies, ma'am?' I inquired. 'No,' she said. 'I suppose the closest I ever came to it was when I knighted Sobers.'

For a couple of irreverent seconds, I almost suspected the Queen of name-dropping, and if that were so, then it was the greatest name of all to drop. John Arlott once painted a memorable picture which hinted at the appeal of the man. 'Everything he did was marked by a natural grace, apparent at first sight,' wrote Arlott. 'As he walked out to bat, six feet tall, lithe but with adequately wide shoulders, he moved with long strides which, even when he was hurrying, had an air of laziness, the hip joints rippling like those of a great cat.' That was Gary; grace, assurance and a talent so precious as to be quite beyond compare. Every cricketer has a hero, even the gnarled old pro who guards his compliments as jealously as his benefit money. And Gary Sobers was my hero.

CHAPTER THIRTEEN

I played with and against him many times, in Test, county and representative cricket, and my admiration for him grew with the years. A small story will offer a clue to the regard in which I held him. Surrey were playing Nottinghamshire in a mundane county match. We had lost much of the game to rain, they had a lead of around 150 and with only an hour to play there was no time to dismiss them and score the necessary runs. Gary was batting and had started to play a few shots, and at the end of an over I walked across to Robin Jackman. 'Don't even try to get him out,' I said. 'Why not?' said Jackman. 'That's what we're here for, isn't it?' I explained myself. 'If you get him out, we've got to watch the others come in and scratch around. The only thing that'll give us any pleasure out here today is to watch this bloke bat. All right?'

Jackman laughed. 'Do you know,' he said, 'I hadn't thought of that. Quite right, Perce. And don't you try to get him out either.' So we just bowled at him and enjoyed his genius, and at the close of play we walked off in his wake. There was no other cricketer I would have contemplated treating with that respect, but then, there was never a cricketer like Sobers.

Gary was the only player in my experience who was held in awe by every Test cricketer; it wasn't something he expected, rather it was the deference that his nature commanded. I saw it most vividly during that 1974 tour of the West Indies when the abuse was flying, the sledging was completely out of hand and the feeling was the worst I have ever known between two cricket teams. Then a wicket would fall and Gary would come in. He would walk through the cordon of slips and say: 'Good morning, fellers,' and people would get on with the game in respectful silence. Eventually, later rather than sooner, he would be out and the abuse would immediately flare up again as violently as before. Nobody would dream of swearing at Gary, for the gods of the game are far above and beyond such petty abuse.

By a rare and happy chance, he was blessed with an attitude to match his talent. He believed that the game was there to be enjoyed and that the overriding duty of a professional cricketer was to entertain. Dave Halfyard of Notts would tell of days when half-volleys were sent screaming for four and long hops were punished with a pull, and at the end of the over he would walk up to his county captain and apologise. 'That's all right,' Sobers would say. 'It'd be a miserable old game if nobody ever hit a four.' In truth, I always felt that he was rated more highly as a captain than his performance really deserved. Certainly he would lead by example and, being a likeable man, he never had a problem in getting players to work for him. But he was not a great tactician, perhaps because the game came so easily to him that he never felt the need to dissect it. He was always impatient for things to happen. When he was leading Notts and they had a side at, say, forty for four on a green wicket with the ball seaming all over the place, you could see Gary snapping his fingers if another half-dozen overs went by without a wicket falling. Most captains, quite correctly, would stay with the seamers, wait for their wicket, then attack the new batsmen with pace and movement. That was far too clinical for Gary. He would remove the seamers, put on an occasional leg-spinner and hope that the change would work the trick. In his book, to attack was not simply the best way, it was the only way. He was fortunate in having Deryck Murray at his elbow in so many Test matches, for Murray was a coldly calculating professional who knew the game and understood its implications. Down the years, West Indies opponents learned to fear that ominous moment when Murray would breathe into Sobers' ear and the tactics would change from high romance to grinding pragmatism.

In his early years, Gary lived at a pace which would have killed most professional sportsmen. He once took me for a night on the town in Barbados after fielding all day in intense heat. We went to a 'jump-up', a deafening disco where Gary danced until two-thirty and drank like a hero. Next morning at seven-thirty he was spotted at a local sports club, playing an hour of table tennis to work off his surplus energy before going off to the ground to compose yet another large and elegant innings against the tourists. Of the great players, perhaps only Denis Compton and Keith Miller have ever managed to combine their sporting and social life to such astonishing effect, although in more recent times Ian Botham has tried hard to join that exclusive company.

There are many batsmen who were far more difficult to bowl to than Sobers, particularly the people who would embarrass you by jumping outside the leg stump and hitting you through the off-side field, but such embarrassment was usually short-lived, for the technique of such players rarely matched their nerve. Sobers was orthodox, in his batting if in little else. He played everything on its merits; drop a ball short and he would cut, let slip a half-volley and he would punish it with a drive, bowl him a good-length ball with a hint of turn and he would treat it with respect. It is easy to bowl to such players, but a sight more difficult to get them out. And he never seemed to lose his form. I once sat with Rohan Kanhai and watched Sobers bat for an hour in the nets. He had not played the game for three or four months, but everything struck the middle of the bat as though it were mid-season. Rohan said that he had played with him for fifteen years and he had never seen him appear out of touch,

CHAPTER THIRTEEN

never watched him endure that period of imperfect timing and uncertain edges which afflicts ordinary human beings.

In addition to his other unreasonable gifts, he was also a superb close catcher. I travelled with him to Karachi in December 1970 to play for the Rest of the World in a match arranged to assist the Cyclone Disaster Fund. I remember bowling to Javed Burki, the Pakistan opener, and after setting the field with me, Gary stood around the corner at leg slip just four feet from the bat, so close that his left foot was on the bowling crease. I waited for him to retreat to a normal position, then I realised that he was going to remain there, legs apart and rubbing his hands together. I got my third delivery to bounce and strike Burki's glove, and suddenly I saw a flash of movement and heard the yell of an appeal. Sobers had pounced, dived and picked up the catch in front of the batsman, where the fielder in the bat-pad position would normally have been standing. It remains to this day the most brilliant catch of its kind I have ever seen.

Sobers never let you down, never fell below the expectations of those who admired him. When we flew out to Pakistan for that match, he spent a large part of the journey playing bridge in the first-class section of the plane. After a couple of hours in his company, Dennis Amiss walked down the plane, bubbling like a fan. 'I might have known it,' he said. 'He plays bridge just like he plays cricket. Everything's big and bold and he goes for all the big shots and he's got style and class and luck as well. I might have known it. How else would he play?'

Perhaps the most remarkable fact of all is that Sobers remained untouched and unspoiled by the universal adulation. In a strange way, he actually enjoyed being brought back to earth by people he knew and understood. Although he appreciated the honour, Gary was not looking forward to the formality which would attend his knighthood. In the event, it was a marvellous day, with the Queen coming to the local racecourse to perform the ceremony and the entire island abandoning itself to the ultimate carnival to demonstrate its feelings for its favourite son. But Gary coped with the formalities, endured the procession of local dignitaries who wanted to pump his hand and address him as 'Sir Gary' and resigned himself to having his back slapped by everybody who could reach him. And at the end of the busiest day of his life, he escaped from his entourage and retreated to a bar for a quiet drink. Outside, the fireworks were bursting, the calypsos were booming and the population of Barbados was chanting the name of Sobers over and over again. Inside, Tom Spencer the English umpire was sitting and supping, enjoying a winter holiday. Gary glanced down the bar and

*The Lord's Test of 1976.
England v. West Indies.
And for twenty memorable minutes,
a cricket match
seemed the least important thing
in the world*

his mouth dropped open. 'Tommy Spencer!' he said. Tom took another swig, looked up and said: 'Hello, mate, what are you doing with yourself these days?' Sobers still chuckles when he tells the story. It was the highlight of his day.

Gary Sobers: to have shared his company was a pleasure and to have played in his generation was a privilege. The happiest claim I can make for my own career is that I played in the same age and on the same field as the greatest cricketer who ever lived.

Chapter fourteen

A bunch of chimps were worth six times as much as a Test cricketer

Until the advent of Kerry Packer, there was a widespread assumption among the men who ruled the English game that cricket should remain untainted by finance. Nobody actually said that cricketers did not deserve to be paid, but you knew they believed that wages were an optional extra, like power steering or a heated rear window. This Edwardian attitude persisted into the mid-seventies, a feeling that cricket was an endless procession of golden summers, good fellowship, splendid sport and, for some, the opportunity to carry the word to the distant corners of the Empire. Why vulgarise such an idyllic existence with considerations of cash? The message that cricketers came cheaply was received and understood by the wider world of commerce, as I discovered when I was asked to open a supermarket in Ewell. It was not a glamorous affair, but it was undemanding; I cut a tape, posed for a few pictures, pushed a trolley around the shelves and reported at the manager's office for my fee. 'Is twenty-five pounds enough?' he said, a little doubtfully. 'I suppose so,' I said. So he shrugged and counted out the notes. 'I only asked,' he said, 'because I tried to get the Brooke Bond chimpanzees to perform the ceremony. But their manager wanted £150.' Suddenly I knew my place. On the open market, a bunch of chimps were worth six times as much as a Test cricketer.

Until the situation changed, however, we had to supplement our incomes as best we could, and one method was the private cricket tour. I had not been selected for the home Tests against India and Pakistan, nor, to my intense disappointment could I find a place on England's tour to Australia. So when Derrick Robins came up with the offer of a seven-week trip around the smaller islands of the West

CHAPTER FOURTEEN

Indies for a fee of £500 — in effect a long holiday with pay — it seemed like a civilised way to round off 1974.

Robins was a monumentally wealthy businessman who was fascinated by sport. He had come to the public's notice during the sixties when he presided over the revival of Coventry City Football Club, but his deepest love was for cricket. He made little secret of the fact that he saw himself as the saviour of international cricket, the driving force behind a new order which would see South Africa, with whom he had close and long-standing connections, restored to the place she once enjoyed. There were those, a few, who believed that Robins possessed Churchillian qualities; others felt that his style owed more to Captain Mainwaring of the Home Guard. My own assessment fell somewhere between those extremes, but there were times during that tour when I found myself unaccountably whistling the theme tune from Dad's Army.

Robins set the tone from the first day, when we assembled in his suite at the Post House at Gatwick and he addressed his fifteen players. He told us that Trinidad had cancelled their invitation to the touring party because of his connections with South Africa. This followed the lead set by Guyana two weeks earlier and meant that we were losing a large slice of our programme. After a night on the telephone, he had made fresh plans. We would fly to Barbados, who were still holding out a welcome, wait for the story to break in the morning papers and then trust that the other islands would agree with the attitude of Barbados rather than with Trinidad. Somebody started to ask the obvious question: 'What if . . .?' Robins cut them short and produced his master plan. If the rest of the Caribbean should be foolish enough to reject us, then we would fly down to Caracas for one match, travel on to Rio for a couple of games then cross the world to South Africa, who had just offered us a full itinerary. He had obviously spent an extremely busy night on that telephone. In the event, the global strategy was never invoked. We were accepted, the West Indies tour went ahead, and I never did get to see Rio.

Robins was a curiously complex character who was, for a time, a man of real importance in the game with his wide-ranging contacts and his personal drive. He could be a likeable man, a generous host and the life and soul of any party. But having paid your tour fee and all expenses, he felt he owned you, body and soul. In fairness, he had chosen some wonderful eccentrics for his touring party. There was, for instance, John Jameson, who attacked life immoderately in the manner of Olly Milburn. John enjoyed a social drink to such an extent that his weight had soared beyond eighteen stones, and this tour offered endless opportunity for social drinking. I remember one game when he walked to the wicket in a drowsily delicate condition, having supped a skinfull during the previous evening. When he came to take guard and the umpire asked him what he wanted, his response was instinctive. 'Rum and coke, please,' he said. Roger Tolchard was another player with whom I had toured at Test level; an adequate wicket-keeper, an excellent player of spin bowling, yet sadly accident-prone. It was on that Robins tour that he showed me a picture of a girl he met when he played in East Africa. She was a stunningly beautiful lady whose attractions were enhanced when she agreed to have dinner with Tolchard. He booked a discreet restaurant, selected the best table and prepared for his romantic evening by spending the afternoon scuba-diving. It proved a great mistake. When he removed the mouth-piece from his breathing apparatus, his false teeth, necessitated by an earlier sporting accident, jerked from his mouth, spiralled down through the water and were lost forever in the sands of the ocean bed. The assignation was not a success. Dinner was fine and the band, apparently, was excellent, but the heavenly creature could not understand a word of the sophisticated conversation which Tolchard mumbled through a row of shining gums.

Characters like Jameson and Tolchard helped to make much of the tour a great pleasure, but you were never allowed to forget that Robins was footing the bill and was therefore calling the tune. We played one game in Dominica, where it rained incessantly. The umpires inspected the wicket and agreed that cricket was impossible, but said that they would delay calling it off for the day until the local mayor had paid an official visit at noon. Robins arrived soon after the scheduled start at eleven, walked five yards on to the ground, announced that it was perfectly fit for play and, after a few brusque words with the reluctant umpires, sent us out to the field. Conditions were so bad that Tolchard kept wicket in a puddle which completely covered his boots. We played a farcical match; splashing, skidding and squelching through a parody of real cricket.But Robins had paid for his entertainment, and he would not be denied.

Yet when it came to socialising, Robins became one of the lads. As with all cricket tours the level of humour was largely schoolboy, rising occasionally to the level of undergraduate. We instituted a Saturday Night Club, which was a transparent excuse for serious drinking, and every week we elected a new chairman. Silly fines were levied, I was repeatedly fined for having been born in Wales, and the stipulated dress varied according to the chairman's whim. In my brief reign as chairman I decreed that each guest should wear swimming trunks, tour ties and a blob of shaving foam, the size of a walnut, upon the end of his nose. The decree was scrupulously obeyed and the hotel guests witnessed the sight of some celebrated cricketers — Mike Smith of Middlesex, Mushtaq Mohammad of Northants, Bob Cottam of Hampshire and many others — clutching armfuls of bottles and praying that the foam would not drop from their noses until they reached the party room.

But the most memorable party of the tour was held in the Holiday Inn in Barbados, when Robins kicked Phil Edmonds through a window. Edmonds was a comparative newcomer to major cricket, but already he was a man of firm and independent views and he would make no concessions to the hectoring style of Robins. Over the weeks they argued about everything; politics, religion, high finance and cricket, and never once were they guilty of agreeing. Much drink had been consumed on the night of Phil's chairmanship of the Saturday Night Club, and the argument between them was raging more fiercely than usual. Eventually, Robins became exasperated beyond control and he playfully kicked out at Edmonds as they sat on a bed. Phil flew backwards, through the net curtain, through the large picture window and on to the balcony outside the room. We were terrified. At best, we feared that Edmonds had been cut to ribbons in that shower of glass. At worst, England had lost the services of an immensely promising left-arm bowler. Then Phil walked back through the balcony door, drink in hand and flicking off slivers of glass. 'As I was saying before you got silly about it,' he said, and continued the argument where he had left it. Robins just chortled. 'You're all right, old son,' he said. 'Nothing wrong with you. Have another drink.'

During that trip, Robins told me that he wanted me to join his team to tour South Africa just a few weeks before the start of the English season. I thought about it, but I knew what my decision would be, and when we got home I wrote to inform him that I was unavailable. Refusal was something he could not understand and he called me several times to check my sanity. Yet I knew what I was doing. Derrick Robins was in many ways a likeable man of extraordinary qualities whose main concern was the welfare of cricket. But I had spent seven weeks coping with the contrasting moods of Winston Churchill and Captain Mainwaring. I felt I had served my time.

Chapter fifteen

Our fellows got carried away

'TODAY, I do believe,' said Trevor Bailey, 'that I have seen a bowler who is possibly even faster than Frank Tyson.' He looked to me for confirmation, since I had just returned to the Lord's pavilion after fending off a few overs from the man in question. Unfortunately, I was unable to debate the point. I had never seen Tyson at his peak, but neither could I claim to have seen many of the balls that Michael Holding had bowled to me that evening. I was at least grateful that the two deliveries which were potentially the most lethal were also the ones I had chanced to see most clearly; two beamers which slipped from his hand, whistled past my shoulder and smacked into the gloves of the distant wicket-keeper. For the rest, it was largely a matter of hope and trepidation, and I survived until close of play through the powers of luck and prayer. The older pundits, from the safety of the grandstand, declared that the spell which Holding had bowled was probably the fastest ever seen in the history of Test cricket, and I readily accepted that judgement.

I had been away from international cricket since that Trinidad Test of 1974 when England recalled me for the second match of the 1976 series against the West Indies. At the age of 28 I was entering my prime as a spin bowler, yet to an English Test crowd I was little more than a rumour. Of the fifteen Test matches I had played to that point, only one had been staged at home, and I was therefore a player whose performances were conveyed by newspaper and radio reports and small snippets of television coverage. I was naturally delighted at the chance to prove myself to a domestic audience, but I knew that this West Indies side was not designed to make my re-entry a comfortable affair. Never noticeably short of fast bowlers, they were

CHAPTER FIFTEEN

now able to perm any three or four from the list of Holding, Andy Roberts, Wayne Daniel, Vanburn Holder and Bernard Julien, and while they had lost Sobers from their constellation of outstanding stroke-makers, they had come up with one Vivian Richards, a Test player for barely two years but a man who dominated that scorching summer with an ease rarely seen since the age of Bradman.

It came as some small mercy to discover that injury had ruled Richards out of the Lord's Test, but the players who remained were much more than adequate. We scored some minor triumph in that we actually took a first-innings lead, then, late on Friday evening a lifting ball from Holding damaged the hand of England's opener Barry Wood, and I was sent out to survive. Wood offered me the equivalent of the hearty breakfast which condemned men are said to enjoy. As we crossed on the pavilion steps, he clutched his injured hand, glanced quickly back at the scene of the accident and mumbled: 'Sorry, Perce.' Long before the conclusion of my first over, I knew that the rumours had been correct, that the man was as fast as his reputation and that he was bowling at a pace which I had not considered feasible. The fact that I did survive and that rain washed out Saturday's play left me with two full days to contemplate the pleasure of facing Holding and his chums once again. But on the Monday morning Andy Roberts quickly put me out of my misery, David Steele and Brian Close put together a couple of solid innings and we finished with a creditable draw.

With England having held such a side to two draws, there was a degree of misguided optimism in certain quarters before the Third Test at Old Trafford. Surely Tony Greig's miserable run with bat and ball could not continue, and surely Frank Hayes would play the big innings he was still threatening and wasn't it inconceivable that Richards could carry on scoring runs at such an immoderate rate? When I looked at the wicket on the first morning, I sensed that the optimism was hopelessly misplaced. It was green and nasty with sinister bare patches; worse, it was an undulating wicket, making the bounce dangerously unpredictable. Bowlers of brisk medium pace would be playable, but it was best not to dwell upon the possibilities for genuinely fast men. I looked again at the respective sides; they were putting out Holding, Roberts and Daniel, we were responding with Mike Hendrick and Mike Selvey, who was winning his first Test cap. Both were fine bowlers of their type, but Brian Close was not being excessively unkind when he described it as a contest between 'their cannon and our pea-shooters'.

In fact Selvey, in particular, bowled beautifully during the West Indies' first innings and captured four wickets as we dismissed them for 211. But even as we were bowling them out, we were thinking

*England v. West Indies at Manchester, 1976 . . .
Brian Close carried courage to the borders of insanity,
yet there were times when his knees buckled and he almost fell*

about what they might be capable of on this wicket. The fears were spectacularly confirmed and their speed was overwhelming. The undulations of the wicket played their expected part; when a ball hit the up-slope on that pitch, it took off almost vertically, when it struck the down-slope, it shot along the ground. England were dismissed and destroyed for seventy-one runs, a score made even worse by the ease with which Richards, Gordon Greenidge and an accomplished supporting cast then helped themselves to 411 for five before declaring and leaving England to bat through the last eighty minutes on Saturday evening.

Those eighty minutes were the most appalling and unforgiveable that I ever saw during all my years in first-class cricket. For some cricketers, they were literally unbelievable. Barry Wood was in hospital for an operation and he woke up, turned on his television and watched Close and John Edrich attempt to defend themselves against Holding, Roberts and Daniel. 'I was sitting up in bed, ducking and swaying,' he said. 'I thought they must be showing the edited highlights. I couldn't believe they were bouncing every ball past our lads' noses. "They're just showing the bouncers," ' I thought. 'Then I realised it was live. Terrifying.' Close was one of the strongest men, both physically and mentally, who ever played the game, a man who carried courage to the borders of insanity, yet there were times when his knees buckled and he almost fell. There was no obvious desire to get him out, the bowlers wanted to knock him out. The English players sat in silence in the dressing room; some were unable to watch. At Old Trafford you view the game from sideways on, and it always seems faster from that position. But to see the bowler start his run at one end of the ground and to see Deryck Murray standing farther back than I have ever seen a wicket-keeper stand and to see Close in the middle, straight-backed and knowing that almost every delivery was bowled with the intention of damaging him was an experience which nobody at Old Trafford on that July evening will ever forget. I was night-watchman and I was more pumped up than I have ever been. After a while, I sat on the balcony outside the dressing room to be closer to the action. I even put on my gloves, a thing I never did until I was on the way to the wicket, and I heard myself muttering: 'Come off, Closey, you've had enough. Come off now, Closey. Let me go out there.' I never stopped to think how a player of my tail-end talent might fare against bowlers who were currently assaulting a class batsman, I just wanted to get him out of it. Mercifully, I was not needed, Close and Edrich survived the full eighty minutes until stumps and when they came in the whole dressing room stood back and stared in genuine awe. Suddenly, Edrich broke into a great gust of laughter. He was looking across the ground at the scoreboard and it amused him enormously. 'D'you know what your score is Closey?' he said. 'One! All that for one! Closey, was it worth it?'

Close was still chuckling when he removed his shirt. The bruises were already beginning to overlap across his chest and ribs, in places there were small clusters of livid bumps, as if somebody had forced handfuls of marbles beneath his skin. The bruising continued all around his body and Bill Ridding, the English physiotherapist, winced at the sight. 'I don't like the look of that, Brian,' he said. 'You'd better get off to hospital for an X-ray.' Close snorted, in the true tradition of Yorkshire heroes. 'Nay, lad,' he said. 'Just give us a Scotch.' He swallowed it at a gulp, limped off to the shower and began to make plans for an evening out. On the Monday morning, I walked into the dressing room and saw Close stripped to the waist while the physio applied a huge piece of chiropody felt to that enormous chest which was mottled by weals and blotches. 'Closey, you're getting soft,' I said. 'Nay,' he said, 'but if I get 'it here again, it might be a little bit tender, like.' The man's courage was absurd, but we all knew that it should not have been tested to that terrible degree. Holding had been belatedly warned for an excess of bouncers and the West Indies captain Clive Lloyd conceded that his bowlers had gone too far: 'Our fellows got carried away,' he said. 'They knew they had only eighty minutes that night to make an impression and they went flat out, sacrificing accuracy for speed. They knew afterwards that they had bowled badly.' In fact, it had been the most disgraceful exhibition of intimidatory bowling that I had ever seen, complemented by an equally disgraceful umpiring performance by Bill Alley and Lloyd Budd who unfortunately was standing in his first Test. Cricket took a long stride backwards on that ugly evening at Old Trafford.

It was instructive to observe how the other England batsmen reacted to the whole affair. They were quiet, thoughtful and apprehensive. Somewhere among those emotions, there may have been a grain of fear, especially as there were no helmets around in those days, but it was less a physical fear than a worry that their technique would prove inadequate. When a man becomes good enough to bat for England, he has evolved a technique for every situation; he knows how he is going to combat in-swingers and out-swingers, off-spinners, leg spinners and left-armers. And he knows how he is going to deal with pace. Now if he is struck on the head, he knows his technique is frail, he has a chink in his armour, and that is the real worry. The usual solutions are no longer relevant. He may duck or hook or sway out of line, but on that pitch and at that pace, chances were that he would still be hit by the rearing ball. So

CHAPTER FIFTEEN

Cricket at
the sharp end . . .

Intimidation
has become
a way of life,
even for tailenders.
I survived
the assault of
Malcolm Marshall
at the Oval in 1984
and I also, narrowly,
survived . . .

. . . Michael Holding bowling the most vicious delivery I ever received at Old Trafford in 1976. The old codes had been abandoned, the game had changed, and I feared for its future.

112

one by one the batsmen walked out to face the ultimate examination in the full knowledge that they had no answers to the most critical questions.

My own slender batting technique had proved hideously fallible on the first evening of the match when I went out to join Edrich as night-watchman. Holding and Roberts were in full cry, and I can remember Edrich saying to me at the end of the over: 'Which one do you fancy, Percy?' It was a choice between hanging and the electric chair, but with memories of Lord's still fresh, I chose to take Roberts as a light relief from Holding. A couple of balls later, a lifting ball thudded into my shoulder and I started to wonder about my decision. But an over or two later I had to face Holding, and he bowled me the most amazing ball I ever received in my career. It pitched just short of a length, three or four yards further up the pitch than his usual bouncer. My feet were outside off-stump, I was perfectly in line and I expected to play it around the splice of the bat. Suddenly, the ball took off and flew and I can recall flicking up my chin, rolling my head and trying to avoid its wicked path when it gently brushed the tip of my nose like the caress of a feather. Everything seemed to happen in slow motion as my head continued to roll, following the ball on its thirty-yard journey to Murray, watching it nick his glove and tracing every inch of its path through to the sight-screen which it struck with a chilling crack. I looked up at the other end and Edrich was stuffing his batting glove into his mouth, giggling in helpless relief. I looked back at the slips — there seemed to be about fifteen of them since they did not waste men in front of the bat when Holding was bowling to Pocock — and they were staring at me with fear on their faces. They were terrified for me. I had never seen, much less received, such a vicious ball, yet in a strange way it gave me something like confidence, since I reasoned that if he hadn't hit me with that one then he was never going to hit me. He got me out in short order, of course, but I was actually able to walk back to the pavilion, and that was a small victory in itself.

By this time, I was no longer surprised to find a fast bowler firing bouncers at a tail-ender. The old conventions were dead, 'all-in rules' prevailed and if you went out there with a bat in your hand, you were fair game. And it was Holding's first tour to England, so he was determined to make an impact and nothing was going to stand in his way. Yet if you could detach yourself from the menace of the man, you were aware of a magnificent fast bowler. It was David Steele who named him 'Silent Death,' from the way he would glide to the wicket, scarcely disturbing the grass yet generating pace with every stride. There were bowlers such as Wes Hall who would vary their pace, throw in a slower ball and keep you guessing. But when Michael was

CHAPTER FIFTEEN

motoring there was no need to guess; you knew that every ball would be blindingly fast, as fast as any man ever bowled a cricket ball.

Their margin of victory at Old Trafford was a trifling 425 runs, and that represented fairly accurately the difference between the teams. But given some of the methods used to secure that victory, there was bound to be tension between the two sets of players, and this tension was not helped by having to share the same small dining room. When it was all over, we sat in uncomfortable silence in that room. The West Indies players were anxious not to appear to be gloating over their victory, the England players were dazed and naturally miserable after the heavy defeat. Half-way through the meal, I looked up and happened to catch Holding's eye. 'Tell me, Michael,' I called across. 'Did you get any to turn out there?' Holding laughed and his colleagues roared and even Brian Close managed a cautious giggle while clutching his ribs. I could not know it then, but that perky one-liner was to be my last contribution to English Test cricket for some little time. Heads had to roll after such a defeat, and I was not surprised when mine was among them.

Unfortunately, when my head started rolling, it simply gathered pace. And it did not come to a halt for eight long years.

Chapter sixteen

I see you're only booked in for two nights

IT WAS Bernie Coleman, an old friend and the chairman of the TCCB Marketing Committee at Lord's, who advised me to get in touch with Kerry Packer. I wrote a formal letter from a frustrated off-spinner who used to play for England: 'Dear Sir,' it began. 'I wish to apply for the post of cricketer with your organisation. I enclose references from the following Test cricketers (names supplied) and a summary of my career to date.' As the letter was written half in jest, I expected a similarly light-hearted reply, yet World Series Cricket offered me some faint encouragement. They thanked me for my interest, informed me that they would soon be requiring more players and assured me that I would be seriously considered when recruiting time came around.

On reflection, it was probably a daft little gesture, but it illustrated my state of mind at the time. I was almost resigned to the fact that the England selectors no longer placed much faith in specialist spinners, the preference was for pace and for all-rounders who could bowl a good length and contribute the occasional twenty with the bat. I was also missing international cricket desperately, but above all I was anxious to get to Australia. There were youngsters in the second team at Surrey who could talk about their experience of playing at Sydney or struggling with the heat and humidity at the Gabba, yet, after almost fifteen years in first-class cricket, those names remained a distant mystery to me. And anyway, I was fully behind the attempts which Packer and Tony Greig were making to drag cricket into the market place and give players the rewards their talents deserved.

Greig made one basic mistake, which was to start recruiting for

CHAPTER SIXTEEN

Packer before he had relinquished the England captaincy. It was a considerable error and it lay at the root of most of the criticism which he was to receive. But when I turn out my wage-slips, pre-Packer and post-Packer, I know how well he fulfilled his promise to put a great deal more money into the pocket of every cricketer. Of course Greig was acting in his own interests and securing his own financial future, but in helping to set up that circus of the world's finest players, he was jolting cricket into an awareness of its own commercial possibilities. After stumbling along for decades, entombed in their own traditions, county clubs were suddenly forced into marketing schemes which would generate the money to pay players who had become aware of their own value. When the Oval first placed advertising boards around the ground, an elderly committee man winced at the sight. 'My God!' he said, 'it looks more like a greyhound track.' He received the obvious answer from a colleague who lived in the twentieth century: 'If it wasn't for those signs, that's just what the Oval would be: a greyhound track.' Some of the Greig–Packer innovations were ridiculed, none more than the idea of putting players in coloured clothing and staging matches under floodlights. Personally I thought it an excellent idea, since it told the world that it was different cricket. If they had played in whites the public might have been persuaded that this was the game we had always known instead of an attempt to invent a slightly different game for a far wider audience. Certainly there have been mistakes and I think the Australians may yet kill the golden goose with their preposterous idea of playing eleven-match finals. This over-kill cynically reduces the status of Test matches, for in effect they are saying: 'We'll play the Tests for you die-hards, but we're really interested in the one-day carnivals which bring in the real money.' If that is allowed to continue then the essential balance will be lost and the game itself will suffer the consequences of excess. But they have got so much right so far that I am confident that the problem will be countered. We are now in the process of sifting through the changes; accepting the good and rejecting the bad. But the tide will never be reversed, things will never again be as they were. When the whole Packer business erupted, the popular cry was that Tony Greig had betrayed the game. I never believed that and I think history will be kind to him. Far from betraying it, I fancy he may just have saved it.

I never did get to Australia, which was far and away the greatest disappointment of my career. I would have sold my soul for a chance to be in Melbourne for the Centenary Test in 1978, the match which followed Tony Greig's triumphant tour of India. But in those pre-Packer days the selectors relied on pace supplemented by the spin of Derek Underwood, and there was a spin bowler who was never going to let down any Test team. Underwood was a strange man in that he grew old before his time. He always had a supply of small talk, which made him a great asset at obligatory cocktail parties. We would wind him up, point him at the Governor-General's wife and friends and he would natter away quite happily for an hour or so. And when the party was over, they would all agree that they had just met an extremely pleasant young man. They were right, of course, since he is one of the nicest men who ever played Test cricket, but in his early years he was an earnest, intense, line-and-length companion. Over the past ten years his interests have widened and greater confidence has brought through a sense of humour we never knew he possessed, yet still there remains that streak of self-criticism which drove him to become one of history's great spin bowlers. He always called himself a 'low-mentality bowler', in that he churned out the same stuff all the time, chipping away and wearing down batsmen. The fact that he carried out that demanding role better than anybody else never seemed to have crossed his mind. He was different from most spinners in that he would cut the ball with his hand rather than impart spin with his fingers. On the point of delivery his hand would cut down the side of the ball, forcing it to dig into the surface and grip, lift and spin. He didn't spin it a great deal off the top of the surface, and to get the desired movement from right to left he had to get his hand to come over quickly, thus generating speed down the side of the ball. On a bad wicket, one on which he could drill the ball into the pitch, he could be quite unplayable. Not only did he bowl people out faster than anybody else, he didn't give away runs while he was bowling them out. His accuracy was legendary and his control was impeccable. Perhaps the greatest compliment the cricket public could pay him was that they became fully aware of his standards only on the rare occasions when he slipped below them.

No spinner could legitimately complain when Underwood was holding down a Test place, but the same could not truly be said of Geoff Cope, the Yorkshire off-spinner. I first played against him as a fourteen-year-old schoolboy and I thought he threw the ball. My conviction grew firmer with the passing years and his action became a matter of common gossip around the counties. Eventually, he made the Test side and it was at this stage that Ray Illingworth came to Bradford to watch Cope bowl for Illy's former county. I was acting captain of Surrey at the time, and Illy approached me in our dressing room. 'How can you let him get away with that?' he said. 'He's chucking every ball. It's terrible, that is. You'll have to report him.' I said: 'Raymond, you're dead right. Of course he chucks it, and if he

CHAPTER SIXTEEN

were a quick or a medium-paced bowler, I'd do him like a shot. But I'm an off-spinner and he's the England off-spinner and I'm not going to be accused of sour grapes.' In the end, the sheer weight of cricket opinion saw Cope filmed and then banned, as he had to be. I felt very sorry for him. He didn't want to throw, and if you had offered him a fair action he would have seized it gratefully. Like others before him, he paid a heavy price for a bent arm.

I was not the only Surrey player of that period whose talents were making no impression upon the Test selectors. Robin Jackman, who would have been the popular choice of county batsmen for a place in the English attack, constantly hovered on the fringe of the Test team without getting the vote. His hopes were highest just before the Jubilee Test against Australia in 1977 at Lord's. 'I really think they'll put me in for this one, Percy,' he said. 'They won't take me on the tour to Pakistan because they think I can only do it in English conditions, but I think they'll give me a chance this time.' He was selected for the squad and turned up at the Westmoreland Hotel near Lord's with the highest hopes. 'The name's Jackman,' he told the hotel receptionist. 'I'm with the England party.' She consulted her list. 'Ah, yes, Mr Jackman,' she said. 'I see you're only booked in for two nights.' He tried very hard to smile, but it wasn't easy. 'You don't know what you've said,' he told the girl. 'But you're probably quite right.' He had to wait for another three years before the place he deserved came his way.

Surrey's fortunes, meanwhile, were alternating wildly between success and despair. The game was still fun to play, it could scarcely be otherwise with characters like Jackman and Intikhab around. While Jackman was the eternal joker, Inty was possibly the most popular player in modern cricket. Indeed, he passed what is almost certainly the ultimate test of popularity during Pakistan's tour of Australia. England happened to be touring at the same time, and Geoffrey Boycott called Inty to ask him out to dinner. Not only did he extend the invitation, but he actually paid for the meal! Inty was treated with a curious reverence when that story swept around the circuit. Yet with all these pleasant people around, we somehow could not assemble a successful team. Fred Titmus arrived at the Oval to replace Arthur McIntyre as coach for a short spell. His appointment never really worked out, and he felt he was never given the freedom that he needed by the committee.

Even when you have bowled off-spinners for fifteen years you can still learn the craft, but few people are able to give you serious help, so from a personal point of view I was delighted when Fred came to the Oval. He resigned after two years of his three-year contract and during that time gave me just the technical advice I was looking for. I

The record books tell of
Intikhab Alam's brilliant spin bowling
and of large scores made at breathtaking speed.
But the dry facts convey only half the story.
A gentle, chivalrous cricketer
whose modesty failed to conceal an immense talent,
Inty was possibly the most popular player in the modern game.
He was also a treasured friend.

don't think we ever disagreed on off-spin bowling, and it was good to have him there when we came off after each session. Often he would make suggestions of subtle changes in tactics and at other times he would say 'just keep going as you are'. Even when he said this, it was reassuring to know that you were pursuing your job along the right lines. Although I was a fairly seasoned campaigner by now, Fred Titmus was probably the most experienced spin bowler in the world, and his views were very welcome indeed. He gave Surrey an invaluable farewell present by signing Sylvester Clarke, the pace bowler who was to become our most important player. John Edrich finally stepped down at the end of 1977, and our former player Roger Knight returned from Gloucestershire to take over the captaincy only to find the team sinking to sixteenth place in the 1978 Championship, the worst season in the county's history.

As one of the senior professionals, I wanted to discuss the situation with Derek Newton, the chairman of the club. I told him that the most urgent need was to bring Micky Stewart back to the Oval as manager. I pointed out that the attitude of many first-team players was irresponsible, the second-team players were even worse and that if we insisted on cutting corners, the outlook was hopeless. Stewart was marketing manager of a sports company and he had been out of the game for six years, but his heart had never left the Oval and when the appropriate financial noises were made, he was not a difficult man to persuade. Before the start of the season, we took a three-week trip to the Far East, which gave Micky the chance to know the players. His drive, combined with the bowling of Clarke, transformed the atmosphere. Players who had been coasting were moved into overdrive, talent was detected and encouraged to thrive and a sense of purpose replaced the aimless attitude of earlier days. Suddenly Surrey became a professional unit once more, and in the next season we finished second in the championship and reached the final of the Benson and Hedges Cup. The fun was even more enjoyable with a winning team.

After extensive Test match experience, the years of county cricket were inevitably frustrating, yet they were made marvellously memorable by the quirky humour of the men who played the game. David Thomas came into the Surrey side during the late seventies and the Oval dressing room, never the sanest of places, simply abandoned itself to anarchy. Thomas was never really of this world, it was as if he had arrived from another planet and was constantly surprised by the details of everyday living. Soon after he came to Surrey, he borrowed his father's Ford Granada for a night out. When he got home, he told his father that a tyre had punctured and he had changed the wheel by the roadside. Mr Thomas was enormously impressed by this unusual display of practical skill, and next morning he drove to the garage to get the spare tyre repaired. There was no spare tyre. David had removed the offending wheel and thrown it over a hedge. What use was a wheel with a flat tyre hanging on it? To make things worse, he couldn't remember which hedge he had thrown it over. Thomas was Monty Python made flesh, and his grip on reality grew no more secure over the years.

Yet for me, the most poignant story of the county years was the tale of Andy Mack, who was a six foot, six inch, hopelessly unco-ordinated left-arm medium-pacer. Andy was on the staff for a couple of years without convincing the management that he had a real future as a county cricketer. He was eventually told that his performances would come under close scrutiny for a month while minds were made up. We were playing Somerset at Weston super Mare on a flat wicket and Viv Richards was in his most belligerent mood, so much so that he scored 200 before tea. It was a hot day, one of the hottest of the summer and the ball was like a lump of suede after being clattered around the rough outfield. Jackman was standing at mid-on, I was at mid-off and we closed in on Andy as he walked wearily back to his mark. Suddenly he started laughing. 'I've got to bowl with this ball, on this wicket at that bloke who's just scored 200. And I'm bowling for a contract! This is a bloody ridiculous game, isn't it?'

Poor Andy, he never was destined for a county cricket career, and how the point was rubbed in. He went on to Glamorgan and things did not work out for him there. Whenever I started to think I was getting a rough deal from the game, that it was treating me unfairly and not giving me the recognition I deserved, I thought of a young lad I saw sitting by the boundary boards at Swansea. He was eating an ice cream and clutching a scorecard, and on the lapel of his jacket he wore a large plastic badge with the cruel inscription: 'I saw Andy Mack take a wicket.'

Chapter seventeen

Don't go on too long about the cricket

ON THE evening before the Manchester Test match of 1984, the England team gathered for pre-dinner drinks in their rural retreat. Now the dinner is an essential and traditional part of Test match preparation, an occasion on which strategy is evolved, tactics are discussed and an atmosphere of team spirit is created which should sustain the side over the next few days. On this occasion the dinner was a more important function than ever, because England had lost the first three Tests to the West Indies and the series was beyond salvation. As we moved through to the dining room, one of the most famous cricketers in the modern game tugged at my sleeve and issued a jovial warning. 'For God's sake, Perce,' he said. 'Don't go on too long about the cricket. Otherwise we'll never get down the pub.'

With all the triumphs, the joys and the marvellous days which cricket had given me, nothing had prepared me for my return. For those few days in July, I was the happiest man in England. After a gap of eight years and eighty-six Test matches, the selectors had remembered a thirty-seven-year-old off-spinner who was still taking a few wickets for Surrey. In the history of the game, only Les Jackson and Derek Shackleton had endured a longer wait between Tests and, rather than blunting my taste for combat, the years of exile had sharpened my appetite for the real thing. I knew that the experience would be brief, for after serving his sentence imposed for touring with the 'rebels' in South Africa, John Emburey would almost certainly return for the following English season. But I was determined to savour every moment, and as I walked out with England on that first morning, several of the kindly Lancashire members called out encouragement. I had always found the Old

Trafford crowd one of the warmest in the country and today they made me feel like a friend.

I had inspected the wicket with the calculation of an old pro. It was a fine pitch, an excellent batting wicket, but I knew it would break up late in the game. If I wanted to make a real impression, then I would need the West Indies to bat last. The coin went up, they won the toss, and my hopes began to evaporate. Then the nerves started to crowd in. I came on for my first spell in eight years and bowled poorly; twelve overs, no wicket for forty-nine. In the nicest way possible, they were carting me around the park. The calculations began again. England had picked me in alliance with Nick Cook of Leicestershire for this Test, but in the next match, at the Oval, there would be scarcely room for one spinner on that unresponsive pitch. West Indies were looking increasingly like a team who would not need to bat more than once, so if impressions were going to be made, then this was the innings in which to make them. It was the tea interval, and a summary by Richie Benaud which brought home my mistake. 'Pat Pocock is the most experienced man out there, but he's feeling the pressure like everybody else,' he said. I realised I had been trying too hard, so I relaxed and bowled tightly and the flow of runs dried up. On the following day, the rewards came in the form of four wickets for 121 off forty-five overs. The crowd was kind, the pundits were flattering and I had satisfied my own expectations. But my happiness was tainted by the loose remark at the pre-match dinner: 'We'll never get down the pub.' I worried about the comment and the attitude it represented and my suspicions were to be confirmed.

On that Friday evening, I approached David Gower and asked the captain if I could have a chat with him on the way home. We arranged to stop off at a pub in Altrincham, and in a quiet corner of the saloon bar I poured out my worries.

I told him that I might be speaking out of turn, that I had been off the scene for a long time and that I had never played Test cricket with any of the current side. But I had to say something as I had never known a more shoddy and apparently uncaring attitude in a Test team. 'Cricket is their last consideration,' I said. 'Nobody even talks about the game. We're three Tests down, we're being stuffed out of sight and some of them don't seem to care about it.' I pointed out that I had played in several eras of English Test cricket; from Barrington and Graveney, to Lewis and Edrich, to Greig and Brearley, and through to the modern side. I had played in one or two great Test teams, a lot of good ones and a few indifferent sides, but never in a team where some players didn't seem to mind whether they won or lost. One or two people wandered into the bar and recognised us but they also recognised the fervour with which the veteran off-spinner was laying down the law to the captain of England. There were no requests for autographs that evening. David accepted my criticism like the civilised man he is. I think he believed I was one of the old school who was speaking from the standards of an earlier generation, but he told me that it was interesting to hear a new point of view from somebody who had been away from the Test game for so long and that he knew I had the welfare of the team at heart. There was no resentment, he conceded some of my points and rejected others. But of the main thrust of the criticism he said: 'I know these people well. They've played a lot of cricket, they're facing the best team in the world and they're tired. Some of them may not look as if they're trying, but they're concentrating more than you think. Deep down, they're trying like hell.' That was his view and one I should have expected from the England captain. But when I saw him pull the side together on the subsequent tour of India and saw the attitude shift so dramatically from being the worst of my experience to the best I had ever known, I knew I had been right on that evening in Altrincham.

I told Gower that in my view the light-hearted approach of Ian Botham was having far too strong an influence on the side. This was scarcely a revelation to the captain, since he must have been aware that Botham was at once his greatest asset and his most significant problem. Although I had known Ian on the county circuit for a decade, I had never experienced his effect on a Test dressing room and I was very disappointed by his attitude. For obvious reasons of talent and ability, the younger players looked to Botham above all others to set them an example of how to handle the problems of Test cricket. They must have been utterly bewildered by what they saw. Being a great player, he could turn on performances of fire and aggression and reap the odd reward in terms of runs or wickets, but all too often he gave the impression that the game at this level was a cavalier affair and that the people you were playing were not really opponents but amusing companions over a pint or three. The team seemed to revolve around his unpredictable moods, and I remembered the story Robin Jackman had told me about his performance as captain in the West Indies three years earlier. Every player regarded Botham as the man who was never beaten, but he came back to the dressing room one day after getting out to Michael Holding who had bowled at blistering pace, quietly put his bat down in the corner and said: 'I'm sorry, I can't play against that sort of thing.' According to Jackman, one thought ran through the minds of the entire team: 'If he can't play it, what chance have we got?'

Botham's influence had not dimished at the time of Manchester '84, indeed, players have told me that it was never so bad before or since. Although Allan Lamb had a successful series, I believe he was suffering from Botham's attitude, as was Paul Allott, and even David himself was affected by the raucous and turbulent personality in his charge. What worried me particularly was the effect which such an approach might be having on the younger players, men like Graeme Fowler, Richard Ellison and Chris Broad who were trying desperately to establish themselves as Test players and might easily have been nudged into adopting an irresponsible attitude towards the game.

In fairness, I am quite sure that Ian had no idea of the impact he was making on impressionable players. He never could understand why others could not perform the kind of feats which he would reel off almost to order. I genuinely like the man. I have been very disappointed by his unprofessional approach on many occasions, but you could not fail to like a man who is rarely half-hearted, never the slightest bit selfish and is always true to his own nature. I can forgive him almost anything for the way he plays the game, a way which the meaner-minded critics will never comprehend. In this respect, if in few others, he reminds me of Ted Dexter, who was frequently abused for getting out between fifty and a hundred when he was seemingly set. That happened to be the way Ted played cricket; he put himself on the line, took the kind of chances which others would decline and ultimately would win a side far more games than he lost. So it is with Botham. When he's batting he looks for all the extravagant shots. When he's bowling, he's trying everything all the time: inswingers, outswingers, bouncers and yorkers, every variation in the book. He is on the attack from the moment they hand him the ball. That is the way he plays, and that is the way he lives, which is why the public want to watch him above all others. I am quite sure that he drives a car, or even flies a helicopter, in that manner, and I know from experience that he plays golf with exactly the same attitude as he plays cricket. He has yet to cope with the concept of the safety shot. You will never see him drive the ball to the centre of the green when the pin is tucked up against the bunker. Instead he will lash it like fury, get it as high as he can and pray that the ball will come to rest next to the pin; always the big shot, always the gamble. I played a week's golf with him at La Manga and all the familiar traits revealed themselves. He had to play for a substantial side-stake to work up a competitive interest, and although he was a nine-handicap golfer, after a couple of rounds he felt able to take on the world. Manuel Ballesteros was forced to play extraordinary golf to contain him, and later he told me that Botham was the longest amateur hitter he had ever seen. 'The man is a gorilla,' he said, unconsciously quoting the famous nick-name. 'He hits the ball as far as Sevvy, yet he doesn't know how to use his legs. If he ever finds out, the ball will disappear.'

CHAPTER SEVENTEEN

As a county cricketer, he is eternally infuriating to colleague and foe alike, since his methods are entirely individual. When Botham was at the height of his powers at Somerset, I occasionally found myself feeling rather sorry for players like Nigel Popplewell; earnest and determined yet untouched by that streak of erratic genius which Botham possesses. Popplewell may have been in for an hour and a half, grafting for forty runs, when Botham would enter, score twenty-eight off his first two overs then hole out to extra cover. Popplewell would wonder why, with all that ability, Botham could not temper his instincts and put together a large and responsible innings. But the world would say the same of Viv Richards, Barry Richards and to a lesser degree even Gary Sobers. Genius not only makes its own rules, it wins more matches than the efforts of honest journeymen. Personally, I would want to play in the same Test side as Botham, even when his attitude was at its most erratic, but I'm not too sure I should want to play in the same county side. He worked hard for Somerset, but towards the end he never seemed to have the burning desire to play for the county, especially after losing his captaincy, nor the same full-hearted drive which had characterised his early championship cricket. Certainly he tried, but there is little doubt that he tried far harder for England, and that is understandable. Most of his fame and much of his fortune had come from his Test performances and it was increasingly difficult to find the same motivation for the more mundane county game. I believe that his decision to leave Somerset was not only timely but inevitable, and I am sure all parties eventually will gain from it.

I found myself wondering, during that Manchester Test, how some of the eminent figures of earlier eras might have coped with the problems which Botham's nature presented. Kenny Barrington would have got on with his own game, then chosen his moment to take his man to one side and offer serious advice. Tom Graveney would have reacted far more aggressively. As a professional of the old school, he would have been affronted by any player, however gifted, who did not share his code. Tom and Ian would have been oil and water. Colin Cowdrey would have found it extremely difficult to cope with Ian, indeed, the very thought conjures a picture of a toddler taking a large and frisky bulldog for a walk. Brian Close could have handled him, as once he did at Somerset, but it may well have involved a certain amount of physical threat from a man who used to chase Fred Trueman around the Yorkshire dressing room at regular intervals. Mike Brearley handled him best of all, although Botham had yet to reach his truculent peak at that stage of his career, but Gower did as well as most when Botham was at his most awkward.

On a personal level, I was reasonably satisfied with my

*Ian Botham . . .
rarely half-hearted,
never selfish and always true to his own nature*

CHAPTER SEVENTEEN

performance on my return to Test cricket. I knew that I was on borrowed time and that at thirty-seven, the selectors would not be looking at me beyond the next few months and possibly not even beyond the next match, so I lingered over every detail; the nets, the fielding practice, the dressing-room chat, even the Cornhill sponsors' tent where old players would gather at the end of the day's play. I wanted to remember everything. I even walked off very slowly after taking four wickets, since I remembered the story of Sadiq Mohammad. He once played a large and splendid Test innings in England, and on his way back to the pavilion, the whole ground rose to applaud him. Twenty-five yards short of the steps, he suddenly stopped and sat on his bat for a few moments. He did not apologise: 'I heard that noise and realised it was all for me,' he said. 'I just wanted to take it all in.' A four-wicket performance scarcely merits a standing ovation, but I knew just how Sadiq must have felt. Yet England were heading inexorably towards an innings defeat, and the general air of jovial indifference was still troubling me enormously.

On Sunday evening, I called Alec Bedser, the former chairman of selectors, in his hotel room and asked if I might speak to him. I had come to know him well over the years at Surrey and, although he remained a selector, he was the only available person with whom I could discuss the situation frankly and in strict confidence. It was a blistering day and he was lying on his bed watching television in thick underpants almost down to his knees. We spoke for two hours and he understood the points I was making and agreed with most of them. He knew all too well that there was no unity of purpose in the team and that the attitude of two or three players was adversely affecting the others. All I was doing was confirming his long-held opinion. The whole situation was alien to Alec's view of the game. Cricket was the only thing in his life, and had been for more than half a century. His devotion to the game was absolute, and it was that quality which had made him such a renowned Test bowler. I knew that he was frequently dismissive of the modern game and that his cricketing gods were the great men of the thirties, forties and fifties, but his principles were sound and his concern for the welfare of the game was keen and genuine. Nothing I told him would have forced him to act, since his loyalty to the chosen captain was total, but the force of my feelings was too strong to control and I wanted Bedser to have the information which might have improved affairs in the long run.

In the short term, there were very few options available to the England side, other than to work harder than ever and seek to avoid the first whitewash in a five-Test series in England. I was chosen as the sole spinner at the Oval and I actually noticed a curiously marked

*Alec Bedser . . .
His dedication to the game has been absolute
— for more than half a century.*

CHAPTER SEVENTEEN

improvement in the side's attitude following Old Trafford. But we were caught on the fastest and bounciest wicket of the series, and once again I marvelled at the absurd fairness of English cricket. What we wanted was a low, slow turner, and not the pitch we received, a wicket for which Messrs. Holding, Garner and Marshall were duly grateful. They proceeded to bowl at truly terrifying speed with their usual disregard for life and limb, and when I spent forty-six minutes as night-watchman — without troubling the scorers — my harsh estimation of the English attitude was marginally softened by a realisation of the pace they had been asked to contend with. I knew just how severe the ordeal had been when Graeme Fowler came in at the end of his second innings, put his bat down and, as he later admitted to me, thought: 'It's over. I haven't got to bat against them again.' Fowler's courage was beyond question, but after five Test matches against that viciously hostile attack, he was physically and emotionally drained. My own contribution was insignificant. On that pitch I was asked to bowl only eight overs in the match — the West Indian spinner Roger Harper bowled exactly the same number — but I did manage a small niche in history by becoming only the second player to bag a 'pair' in successive England Tests. I often wonder how Mr. R. Peel felt when he set the precedent in 1895.

Despite the increase in effort and determination, the whitewash could not be avoided, but at least the West Indies were now behind us and we could now look forward to something like light relief in the form of the gentle and largely unknown quantity of Sri Lanka at Lord's. But the fates did not intend to let us off so easily. We won the toss, asked them to bat and they responded to the invitation by scoring 491 for seven declared. It was in this game that I became aware of another facet of Ian Botham's extraordinary character. After failing to penetrate with pace, Botham took to lobbing up off-spinners. They started to gorge themselves on Botham's off-spin and in that long first innings he was hit for four an over in the course of twenty-nine overs. Now I have never been a great man for statistics, for when you bowl, as I did throughout my career, in a largely attacking manner, you cannot afford to keep one eye on your figures. But I can remember thinking: 'God, I wouldn't let them smash me around like this. It's not doing his figures much good, is it? But he doesn't seem worried.' Then I recalled that he had already taken 300 Test wickets. With that collection under his belt, anything the Sri Lankans might do would make the most minute decimal-point difference to his enviable average. In truth, he had very little to worry about.

But my abiding memory of that Sri Lanka game was of the gentleman in the Long Room. I had bowled with real economy in the

*David Gower . . .
of the officer class. Confront him with a firing squad
and he would decline the blindfold*

first innings, two wickets for seventy-five off forty-one overs, and some comment had been made on the fact that I was not introduced until Sri Lanka were thoroughly set. This fact had not escaped an MCC member who approached me in the Long Room at close of play. 'Do you realise, Pocock,' he said, 'that you were not asked to bowl until three twenty-nine this afternoon?' I smiled at his concern. 'Don't worry about it,' I said. 'I've been waiting eight years to get back to all this. A few more minutes makes no difference.'

Chapter eighteen

Getting blown away on a cricket field is a bit different

THERE are occasions in the career of every professional sportsman when he finds himself pausing to wonder why a grown man should devote so much time, energy and effort to something as trivial as a game. John Arlott once said that we take sport too seriously and life too lightly, and the truth of his observation came home to me one evening in New Delhi when I sat in a darkened room in the Taj Palace Hotel while a video machine churned out pictures of dying children, burning bodies and homeless, helpless families. I had come to India to play cricket; to take wickets and reinforce my reputation in the twilight of my career. A few hours ago, these had seemed important reasons for travelling across the world, but as I stared at that screen, I felt more than ever like a frivolous intruder.

We had arrived in India in the middle of the night, and those of us who long ago were captivated by the country abandoned ourselves to the heat, the smell, the confusion and the beguiling charm of its chaotic welcome. A few of the newspapers had held their front pages to greet the England team, and when I awoke after three hours sleep, those pages were strewn across my bed with pictures of David Gower blinking through the flash bulbs and promising a memorable Test series. But by then the radio was telling a different, more sombre story. Early that morning, the Indian Prime Minister Mrs Indira Gandhi had been assassinated by her bodyguard. Chaotic charm had been replaced by savage reality, and from my hotel window I could see the armoured cars, the troop carriers, the trundling tanks and all the signs and symbols of a nation gripped by an appalling emergency. I glanced at my bags and wondered if I should start to unpack. Pessimistically, I decided against it.

CHAPTER EIGHTEEN

As ever, I had looked forward to this tour as the one which was destined to be different. There would be no student riots of the kind I had met in Pakistan all those years before, no bottle-throwing as in Jamaica, no threats from Black September which overshadowed the Tony Lewis tour and no sheltering in besieged dressing-rooms as we did on that wild evening in Port of Spain. We had even been given a vote of confidence before leaving London. Peter May, the chairman of selectors, had assembled us in the committee room at Lord's and told us that none of the 'rebels', whose suspension for touring South Africa would soon expire, had a divine right to regain their places in the England side. We were the men in possession and we would be given every chance to state our claims. As panic and retribution spread across the sub-continent and the ominous sounds of civil unrest drifted through the corridors of our elegant enclave, it seemed that those claims would remain unstated.

Speculation grew and prospered. Everybody had a theory but nobody could offer solid information, so we sat by the hotel pool and chattered out our worries, and the newsmen began to arrive. It was only then that the magnitude of what had happened began to overwhelm us. They descended in droves from all over the world; scurrying, questioning, bribing, pleading and doing whatever was necessary to convey the significance of the event which had taken place just half a mile down the road from our hotel. The CBS network of America sent a team of some twenty men and allocated a room just down the corridor from my own to house all their equipment. After a couple of days, the controller of the operation invited me to that room to see the results of their filming, and it was there that I watched those hideous pictures and realised the extent of the tragedy which had seized the nation. The scale of the televison exercise was something I had never experienced. No Indian taxi driver would hazard his vehicle in riot areas, so they bought ten taxis for their crews and hired drivers. On the first day, eight were burnt out by rioters, so they bought ten more taxis the next day on the assumption that two would get through with the pictures. Telephone lines were an eternal anxiety in India, where a single call could involve a four-hour delay. The Americans solved this simply by putting a call through to New York and leaving the line open for days on end, at incalculable costs. In a land of bleak, endemic poverty, they buried each problem beneath a mountain of dollars.

Meanwhile we gossiped and guessed, worked out in the hotel gymnasium, endured the pranks of Allan Lamb and gave grateful thanks that Ian Botham was not on hand to lend his own sense of humour to those doleful days. At last the manager, Tony Brown, emerged from his latest visit to the British High Commission with

*Eden Gardens, Calcutta . . .
where 90,000 passionate partisans
escape the sombre reality of daily life
to enjoy Test cricket*

CHAPTER EIGHTEEN

news that a brief trip to Sri Lanka had been arranged while India was passing through its period of official mourning. The President of Sri Lanka, who had come to Delhi for Mrs Gandhi's funeral, obligingly put the Presidential jet at our disposal and we flew into the daunting heat of Colombo. After the oppressive tension of post-assassination India, the relief was enormous and we played a four-day match followed by a one-day game, which was aborted when fifteen inches of rain fell in four hours and agile local fans could be seen diving into the flooded outfield from the top of the boundary boards.

Thanks largely to the industry of Tony Brown, a re-arranged itinerary for India was assembled. We returned to begin the real business of the tour, lost heavily to the Indian Under-25 side in Ahmedabad and suddenly found ourselves reeling from the heaviest blow of all. Percy Norris, the British Deputy High Commissioner in Bombay, was a good friend. I had met him years before when he held a diplomatic post in Dubai and I visited the country for a single-wicket tournament. His wife, Angela, had been extremely kind to Diane at that time, showing her the sights while I was at the cricket ground, and it was good to meet them again at the party they threw for the team two days before the First Test. Diane was coming out to join the Indian tour within a few weeks and Angela Norris was trying to arrange temporary accommodation for her in Calcutta. When she saw me at the party, Angela asked me to call the High Commission at eight-fifteen next morning with details of Diane's flight plans. It was a good evening in bright, informal company and the players enjoyed themselves thoroughly. Next morning I called as arranged and an aide began to question me suspiciously. Then he broke the news: 'I'm very sorry to tell you, Mr Pocock, that Mr Norris was shot dead five minutes ago.' I remember babbling as one does at such times: 'But I was with him at eleven thirty last night. This isn't the sort of thing you joke about, is it?' His tone dismissed that absurd hope, and he asked me to pass on the news to Tony Brown. As I left my room, I walked past David Gower's door and decided to tell the captain.'Perce, old boy. How are you? Come in,' he said, then I spluttered out my message. He sat down abruptly on his bed and put his head in his hands. 'Bloody hell, Perce. I feel sick,' he said.

I walked downstairs to where Brown, with his assistant Norman Gifford and the physio Bernard Thomas, were assembling the players for the traditional team picture, and I told the three of them together. They were as shocked as Gower had been, but they let the photograph go ahead. Then Brown cancelled the day's practice, called the entire squad to his room and broke the news. The players reacted like a set of punch-drunk fighters. First the Prime Minister, then Percy Norris; who would be next? And this time, the general speculation was tinged with apprehension. The whole party, Press as well as players, wandered about the lobby of the Taj Mahal Hotel, nervously awaiting developments. One or two people suggested going off to practice, but the idea was quickly rejected, and Allan Lamb voiced the thoughts of most of the team. 'One of the leading Britons in this country has just been shot. We don't know who did it or why, but if somebody's trying to make a political gesture we're going to be pretty easy targets.' Tony Brown did not handle the situation skilfully. 'I've got all the passports next door,' he snapped at Lamb. 'If you want to collect yours, you can get the next plane home.' It was our first experience of Brown's short fuse, and the players were not impressed. A short time later, a man I had not met since schooldays approached me in the lobby. He told me that his offices had been closed down and that the British Airways offices, in the same building, had also been closed. I rang Brown's room to pass on the information, thinking that it might help him make a decision. He thanked me, then ten minutes later launched into a fierce tirade at the hotel reception desk. 'I have discovered that the BA offices are not shut,' he shouted. 'I will not have you spreading these rumours and frightening people.' I was about to apologise for my mistake when word came through that the offices had indeed been closed. Brown walked away fuming. The pressure was obviously getting to him. For the rest of the day, the lines between Bombay and London were constantly busy, but the decision was taken to go ahead with the Test match.

Security was intense, police and soldiers were everywhere and while our guardians were numerous, we had certain doubts about their efficiency. The doubts were confirmed on that first morning, when an English photographer in a vast flak jacket with bulging pockets introduced himself to a be-ribboned and be-medalled officer as a representative of the IRA who would like to be taken to the English dressing room. The officer, an obliging man, personally escorted him through a maze of corridors and delivered him to the dressing room door. It was not the most tasteful prank, but it made its point; if anybody seriously intended to despatch an England cricketer, then they could be pretty certain of getting their way.

In my view, and in the view of many players, Tony Brown had acted in a slightly cavalier fashion in deciding to go ahead with the match. He was following the line of the British High Commission, but that did not reassure us since they were offering only educated guesses about the possible consequences. Some players, notably Allan Lamb, believed he had sold us down the river. I did not share that opinion, but I believe he should have asked more questions and extracted firmer guarantees. The fact that we got away with it did not

CHAPTER EIGHTEEN

wholly vindicate his decision. As for David Gower, he remained as laid-back and unconcerned as ever, going about his job as if nothing unusual had happened. 'You've got to go sometime,' he would say. 'And getting blown away on a cricket field is a bit different from dying in bed, don't you think?'

In the end, the team slowly responded to Gower's lead. We entered the game confused, uncertain and laden with problems, but by lunch on the first day, all thoughts of a possible attack had vanished from almost every mind. This was Test cricket and India were a formidable Test team. They would offer us all the problems we needed in the weeks that lay ahead.

*The art of close fielding
improved beyond measure during my career.
The exceptional brilliance of Lock, Stewart and Roope
being matched by today's close-in fielders
who stand in improbable positions
and routinely hold the kind of catches
which an earlier age would have deemed impossible.
The illustration does indeed show India's Srikkanth escaping,
but at the same time allows
Adrian Murrell's exceptional photography
to emphasise David Gower's extraordinary reflexes.
The advances in modern printing technology
have combined three photographs into
one picture of the modern game of cricket.*

Chapter nineteen

We scooped up more oranges and resumed our attack

WE KNEW just what they would be saying back home, and we could scarcely blame them. Whitewashed by the West Indies, embarrassed by Sri Lanka and now beaten in Bombay by India. Old men with long memories racked their brains to recall a time when English cricket had known such disarray. Younger men, with Wisden at their elbows, simply cited the encouraging fact that no Test team had ever won a series in India when coming from behind. A few brave voices searched for justification; the umpiring was appalling, the outside pressures had been unprecedented and the Indian batting had become the equal in depth and quality of the West Indies. But the time for excuses had long since passed. England were hopelessly inept, another humiliation was under way and leader columns and sports pages were as one in cursing the absence of the resting Ian Botham.

If such thoughts ever crossed the mind of David Gower after our eight-wicket defeat in Bombay, then he disguised them quite admirably. The more I saw of Gower, the more convinced I became that nothing could disturb that air of languid self-possession which he presented to the world. Gower was of the officer class. Confront him with a firing squad and he would decline the blindfold: 'Straighten up that line, chaps. And try not to make too much noise with those damned rifles.' In private, he could shout and thump tables when people fell short of his expectations, but he was no martinet, he preferred to lead by example and nudge his players along a more intelligent path. He allowed his men a good deal of licence, but he abhorred stupidity and he chose his moment to chastise it. I still believed that he had allowed things to drift too far in the home series against the West Indies, but I was becoming aware that he was a much harder character than my earlier impressions had suggested.

If Gower was born to the officer's role, then Mike Gatting proved a superb staff-sergeant. Watching them at work was like studying a class batsman in action; Gower's left hand provided the control and the guidance while Gatting's right hand imparted the power and the punch. Gatting was at the very heart of the tour, as important a figure in the team room or the bar as he was on the field. He was an immensely popular vice-captain who threw himself into the business of winning, chuckled his way through the bad times and possessed a skin so thick that it was cheerfully impervious to all the stick which flew his way. Not only did he grow more cheerful as the tour progressed, he actually grew larger. Indian food and drink seemed to suit Gatting all too well and a figure which had never been slender slowly acquired Michelin proportions. I remember Chris Cowdrey coming on to bowl during a large Indian stand in the Calcutta Test while Gatting stood at slip. Discussing field placings with Cowdrey, Gower said: 'As we've only got one slip, would you like Gatt a foot wider?' Cowdrey contemplated the portly character who was doing his best to block out the sun, and he shook his head. 'I wouldn't advise it, skipper,' he said. 'I think he'd burst.'

Gatting's character was a considerable asset to the side, but his batting proved absolutely crucial. On the county circuit, people respected the man as one of the finest batsmen of his generation, yet they were perpetually amazed at his inability to express himself at Test level. He had been dropped once again by England after the Second Test against the West Indies at Lord's when he was twice dismissed while padding up to Malcolm Marshall. We knew he was a far better player than that, and the Indian tour was probably his last chance to prove himself a Test cricketer. Gatting also realised his precarious situation, and one of the authentic consolations from the Bombay defeat was his first Test century in his fifty-fourth Test innings. From that moment, he proceeded to play with the freedom he had always promised, and he went on to indulge his appetite for runs as freely as he indulged his taste for Indian cuisine. There was a tacit assumption that Gatting would one day become captain of England, although his support for Gower was unqualified. Personally, I was not certain that he would prove the ideal choice for the job. I had played against him many times when he captained Middlesex, I had also experienced his captaincy when he had led England in up-country matches and I found him a little dogmatic and inflexible. Gower was frequently criticised for listening to too many people before taking a decision, but that decision was invariably his own. Gatting, by contrast, would take up a set position and nothing would shift him. I preferred Gower's style of leadership, but I could well imagine the day when England might opt for the uncomplicated certainty of Gatting.

Far from being a fatal deficiency, the absence of Ian Botham had much to do with the eventual success of the Indian tour. By some curious English process, adversity had created a sense of communal purpose. In normal times, the team would have looked to Botham to save them with bat or ball, now they were required to stand on their own feet. Even after Bombay, they knew the Indians could be beaten, something which they rarely believed of the West Indians, and with no terrifying pace to be endured this time they were certain that application and hard work could carry them through. All that was needed was a single, solid success ... and Delhi was to prove the answer to our prayers.

I had made a trivial piece of cricket history in the Bombay Test when I walked out alongside Chris Cowdrey and thus became only the second England player after Wilfred Rhodes — who played with both Fred and Maurice Tate — to play Test cricket with two generations of a family. In Delhi, I made a rather more significant statistical contribution when I took three wickets in the first innings then shared eight wickets with Phil Edmonds during India's second innings collapse. The series was level, and we gathered at the British High Commission to celebrate England's revival with a memorable menu of sausages, mash and champagne. By now, team morale had soared to a height I had never experienced in the course of a long career. That spirit was assisted by the comforts of the palatial hotels which the Indians were providing at almost every stage of the trip. I recall Norman Cowans' wide-eyed delight when he saw the enormous room we were to share at the magnificent Rambag Palace at Jaipur. 'Amazing, Perce!' he said. 'D'you know, I could fit my Sunday League run-up into this bedroom.' And he marked out fifteen paces to prove his triumphant point. I was laughing at the way in which cricketers relate everything to cricket when I walked into the bathroom and heard myself say: 'Look at this! It's bigger than most county changing rooms!'

Hyderabad was equally sumptuous, and that, alas, proved to be the place where the old pro forfeited his image as the respectable elder statesman. The hotel was situated by the side of a vast lake. Overlooking the lake was a large terrace on which people would eat dinner and sip cocktails and watch the floodlit fountains which spouted on the small island some fifty yards off-shore. Now the Press had challenged the players to a gondola race around that island. It was to be a serious contest, bets had been struck, lane draws had

*Mike Gatting . . .
One of the most formidable batsmen
and dangerous opponents in the English game*

been made and the journalists had foresworn strong drink for at least an hour before the big event. As the gun cracked and the crews splashed out into the lake, Graeme Fowler and I sneaked away from the large crowd of supporters and made for our room on the eighth floor, where we had laid in provisions. Vic Marks' wife, Anna, had been given £10 to purchase oranges and she had returned with the equivalent of two dustbin loads. We had also filled four huge polythene laundry bags with water and stored them on our balcony. After a few drinks to steel our nerves, we were ready. As the crews steered their erratic course to the shore, shouting, arguing and splashing, we began a sustained bombardment with large, soft oranges. Smith and Lander of Mail and Mirror received direct hits. Woodcock and Carey of Times and Telegraph yelled elegant curses as the missiles splattered their speeding craft. Suddenly, I heard a gasp beside me as Fowler, losing his balance after an enormous heave, started to topple over the balcony. I grabbed his shirt and pulled him back and for a few terrifying seconds we stared at the distant terrace below and realised how close we had come to disaster. 'Thanks, Perce,' he said, and we scooped up more oranges and resumed our attack. Gatting and Cowdrey, then Gower and Bruce French took the rest of the demented barrage as the fans roared and the hotel staff cheered and the stately terrace rocked with the juvenile excitement of it all. Had we left it there, all would have been well . . . but there still remained the water bags. The first two hit the disembarking sportsmen, but the third and fourth split in mid-air, with disastrous results. Two gallons of water drenched a visiting Finnish diplomat who was dining with his wife in the terrace restaurant. A further two gallons struck an Indian businessmen who was inspecting the premises with a view to holding his daughter's wedding reception in the hotel. The joke had misfired in the most shameful manner and the senior pro was in deep trouble.

David Gower then turned on his charm full beam, a not inconsiderable feat since his hair and newly grown beard was matted with orange pith and juice was dripping from his ears. He soothed the Finnish diplomat, explained the unfortunate accident and almost persuaded him to see the dubious joke. The businessman was less easily pacified, and I wrote him a fulsome apology and enclosed one of my two tour ties as a peace offering. I had no idea how he would receive the gesture, but the hotel manager told me that he had returned the following day wearing an England tie, beaming, and bearing an order for a massive wedding reception. In mitigation we could offer only the feeble defence that we had been away from home for a long time and that we had suffered the kind of stress and tension to which no touring team had ever been subjected. The defence was accepted and no action was taken. But the younger players never looked upon their elder statesman in quite the same light after that. It became the most celebrated evening of the entire tour.

Despite these social indiscretions, the balance of cricketing advantage was now tilting firmly towards England. The factions within the Indian side were starting to bicker and separate. Kapil Dev was dropped for the Third Test in Calcutta after throwing his wicket away in Delhi and although intermittent rain ruined the Calcutta Test, Sunil Gavaskar suffered bitter and well-merited public censure for extending the Indian first innings beyond lunch on the fourth day. After the inevitable draw, the chance of an English break-through was beckoning, and that chance was seized in the Fourth Test in Madras. There were some stunning individual performances in Madras, where Neil Foster took eleven wickets in his first game of the series and Gatting struck an imperious double-centry, yet I derived most satisfaction from the innings of my room mate, Graeme Fowler. Because of the nature of the job, cricketers spend an enormous number of hours in each other's company. Occasionally there is friction, mostly they rub along through their shared interest in the game, but sometimes they strike up deep friendships which will outlive their cricket careers. During those crowded months in India, 'Foxy' Fowler became a genuine friend. A Northerner by birth and inclination, he had travelled the world yet remained ferociously proud of his own patch of Greater Manchester: 'where the real people live.' He hated my tapes — which he swore had been recorded from ancient 78's — he cursed my compulsive tidiness and he offered me grave warnings on the dangers of early nights. I deplored his late hours, the noise which he made while searching for his bed and his curious habit of using the carpet as a wardrobe. In short, we got along famously. The one thing which seriously worried him was that nobody had given him sufficient credit for being a fine player. They said he was brave and gutsy and willing, all those terms one uses to describe batsmen who are just short of Test class. He needed a big Test innings to reassure himself, and as the tour wore on, that innings continued to elude him. Before the Madras Test, I spotted a small flaw in his technique. Instead of bringing the bat through straight, he was playing across the ball with an open face so that if the stroke were marginally ill-timed, he would nick a catch to slip. I told him of this in the nets and for an hour or so I threw balls at him as he worked to correct the fault. Then we went to see Gower play shots in the nets, and with that immaculate technique in mind we worked for a further hour. When a player sets himself to cure one fault and feels he has

CHAPTER NINETEEN

succeeded, his confidence often receives a curious boost, and when Foxy went out to bat in Madras, I knew that he was in the mood to achieve great things. When he returned to the room that evening, he had 149 not out against his name. He flopped on his bed, shattered and content, and after a while he took delivery of a telegram from his old Lancashire team-mate David Lloyd who had once scored 214 against India. 'Not bad,' said the wire, 'but you've got to go a long way to beat 214.' Out he went the next day and pushed on to 210 before falling to Kapil Dev. He came in that night and lay on the bed for more than an hour. 'I can't be a bad player, can I, Perce?' he kept saying. 'I know it wasn't 214, but it's a lot of runs, eh? A bad player wouldn't score those, would he? No, I can't be a bad player.' I was never more pleased for anybody than I was for Foxy Fowler that night.

One up with one to play, the tour could by now be counted a sporting success. That it was also a social success was due in large part to the arrival of the players' wives in mid-tour. On my first full England tour, back in 1968, only three wives had joined their husbands in the West Indies. Now they were turning up en masse. It was one of the most civilised advances English cricket had made over the years. People outside the game find it impossible to imagine the strain and stress which prolonged absence places upon a marriage. The Test cricketer's wife knows better than most what it is like to be part of a one-parent family, to cope single-handed with tasks which ought to be shared, to be deprived of adult company and adult conversation and, perhaps worst of all, to sit down to Christmas dinner with the empty chair as a constant reminder. I have known players withdraw into sad, private shells as the strain of absence became intolerable and I have seen strong, confident men break down when they opened a letter and saw the writing smeared by tear drops. The casualty rate of cricket marriages is depressingly high, there was a time when nine of the Middlesex team were either divorced or on their second marriages, and I believe the rate would be far higher if the long absences were unrelieved by a two or three week visit.

In recent years, at least one of the cricketing wives has become something of a celebrity in her own right. I remember having a long conversation with Frances Edmonds one evening in Hyderabad. I had not seen her for some years and I had almost forgotten just how effervescent, witty, opinionated, perverse, outrageous and generally fascinating the lady could be. As I walked back to the team bus, the details of the conversation were still flickering through my mind and I said to David Gower: 'She's a strange girl, isn't she? It's a good job she and Phil chose each other.' 'Yeah,' said Gower, 'saves messing up

*Graeme Fowler . . .
'Foxy' made it,
but he was never sure he had been accepted*

four lives.' I liked the Edmonds' and I enjoyed their company, but I could see precisely what Gower meant. Most of the players kept her at arm's length on that tour; she was, after all, a journalist who was in something of a privileged position. They didn't understand her and that worried them, so they measured their words and stifled their opinions when she was around. They were unused to independent women, particularly when that independence was flaunted in such a pointed fashion. As an immensely gifted linguist who is fluent in four languages, Frances earns a considerable salary for her work as a translator, and she enjoyed the shudder she provoked from players when she referred, as frequently she did, to '*Our* house in St John's Wood and *my* flat in Brussels.' Had she been an outsider, many of the players would have sent her packing, but they could not do that because of Phil's position, and it irritated them. So the unsinkable Frances sailed on; observing, commenting, criticising and remaining completely indifferent to the views of less talented people. I used to think that if I were to draw up a list of pros and cons, then the reasons for disliking her would far outnumber her endearing qualities, yet like her I do because she is shamelessly entertaining and utterly irreverent. She is also one of the few people who can hold her own in an argument with Phil Edmonds.

As Gower had observed, it would take somebody like Phil to be married to Frances, since Phil is one of those people who will start an argument simply to keep in practice. He has an agile mind which apparently needs constant challenge to keep in shape and when he can find nobody with whom to argue, he will dip into his stock of conundrums to kill an hour at an airport or a day in the deep field. Along with the agile mind goes an extraordinary physical power which is rarely apparent to the cricket public. Fred Titmus said that Edmonds was probably the strongest man who ever played cricket, an athlete of restless, driving energy with the mobility and ball sense of the great games player. That energy not only made him a fine cricketer, it also made sharing a room with him virtually impossible. Allan Lamb was his principal victim in India. On nights before a free day, we would go to a reception, sit around in the hotel lounge and retired to bed in the early hours. As Lamb climbed between the sheets, Edmonds would say: 'I suppose you want to turn out the light and go to sleep?' Lamb would swear, very loudly. 'Of course I want to go to sleep,' he'd say. 'It's half past two in the morning.' And Edmonds would sigh, pick up his book and retire to the bathroom. He needed only three hours sleep and he never understood people who required rather more.

From a technical point of view, Edmonds is the best-equipped spinner I have ever seen. He has accuracy, flight, control, confidence and imagination, along with an action which is very high and admirably simple. His two-stride run-up is insufficient to generate pace, but sheer strength allows him to bowl the quicker ball to devastating effect. One of the great joys of the Indian tour was to bowl for long spells in harness with Phil Edmonds and to watch one of the game's great spin bowlers operating at the peak of his powers.

When you have a spinner of the highest quality at the other end, you can work together with a much larger game-plan, and the enjoyment of the strategy is the very essence of what spin bowling is all about. That enjoyment was heightened by the quality of the batsmen who confronted us. Men like Gavaskar, Vengsarkar and young Azharuddin are the finest players of spin bowling in the world and they raised competition to the level of an absorbing physical and intellectual exercise.

In the course of those long and satisfying spells alongside Edmonds, I experienced some of the pleasure which John Emburey has known for much of his Test and county career. Emburey is moving past the stage where he may be regarded simply as a fine international bowler and is approaching that peak of excellence which will see him recognised as one of the most gifted spinners in the history of Test cricket. Such is the nature of the modern game that his figures will tell a false story. He is not destined, I fancy, to gather spectacular hauls of eight or nine wickets, bought at considerable cost, but he will contribute numerous performances of nerveless accuracy. He is seen at his best in one-day cricket when two wickets for 25 off 12 overs will win more games than seven for 75. To watch Emburey rocketing the ball in at the blockhole by the batsman's toes with a control which marginally avoids low full tosses or half-volleys is to witness an off-spinner who has made himself invaluable to the English cause. Yet his batting reveals even more of his character. Emburey is actually a poor batsman, with scarcely a natural stroke to his name, but he has dissected his game, picked on the two or three shots he can play with some success and worked at them with such determination that his reward can be seen both in the averages and in England's successful one-day record. Through sheer force of character, he has made the most of abundant gifts as a spinner and of his fragile talent with the bat to become one of the truly important English players of his era. I wait, with some curiosity, to learn the names of the men who might eventually succeed the Middlesex pair in the England side, for Edmonds and Emburey are so far ahead of the field that their challengers have yet to raise their voices.

An even greater joy was to have, for a few weeks, the company of Diane, my daughter Sami and Toby, my twelve-year-old son. I had called Diane and asked her to warn the children that they were

CHAPTER NINETEEN

coming to a country which was quite different from any they had known. They understood the warning when they flew into Calcutta, with its damp blanket of heat, the huddled masses scratching a desperate living, the stench of cow dung fuelling a million primus stoves and the smoke drifting up into the eternal smog. And alongside abject poverty, the splendour of the Grand Hotel, with its palm trees and its pool, its fine wines and opulent cuisine. I had learned over the years to love the country, but I had also learned to stifle my European conscience.

I was glad that the family had been able to share a part of the tour, because I knew that my days as a Test cricketer were coming to a close. In Bangalore, just ten days before the Final Test, David Gower approached me and asked if he could come to my room for a chat. 'Come on,' I said, 'but I know what you're going to say.' When we got to the room, David gave me the message I had expected. 'I'm very sorry,' he said. 'As you know, we're only allowed to take a group of fourteen to Australia, we think the seamers are going to do it and I'm afraid you and Bruce French won't be coming with us. I will recommend to the Board that a touring party is never split up again, but this time we've got no choice.' Norman Gifford and Tony Brown were equally kind and equally angry about the situation, but they too were powerless to change it. After coming through so much for so long as a team, we were going to be broken up before the journey was over. I felt like a golfer who has failed to make the cut, but I knew there would be no more tournaments, no more days to put things right.

I played in the last Test at Kanpur, but I was dissatisfied with my bowling and at the end of a long day I was in a morose mood when I returned to the hotel. Graeme Fowler immediately sensed my mood and although I was no longer sharing a room with him, he called me into his room where five or six players were listening to tapes. He switched off the music — Dire Straits or Big Country or some such clamour — and dug out a Barbra Streisand album which he knew I liked. He went to his treasured wine box and poured me a large glass, then he cut me a slice of English cheese, sat me in the most comfortable chair and generally fussed over the old fellow. It was a sensitive gesture, carried out without an ounce of show and it said everything about the man.

We drew the Test without discomfort, the series was ours and the subsequent party did full justice to the achievement. But the sadness came crowding in because for me it was all over. We flew back to Delhi, spent twenty-four hours in the capital and travelled to the airport. The England team filed aboard a flight to Sydney and I walked off to wait for the London plane. I didn't sleep much during

*The author as batsman . . .
and the Pocock family, Sami (left), Diane and Toby*

Mrs Frances Edmonds —
journalist, author, linguist and wit
pictured in the company of her cell-mate,
who plays cricket
for England

CHAPTER NINETEEN

the flight, instead I sat there and drifted back through the days of Test cricket. I'd played twenty-five Test matches, I could have played sixty. I *should* have played sixty. But what the hell. How many people get to play in twenty-five Tests? And how many people ever enjoyed them as much as I had?

A couple of weeks later, I watched the highlights of the one-day matches in Australia. In particular I watched Fowler, who was looking nervous and agitated, as if the pressure were worrying him. I turned off the television and wrote him an encouraging letter, talking about his form, passing on some news and asking after mutual friends. At the end of the letter I said: 'By the way, I want you to realise that what you did in Kanpur didn't go unnoticed. I knew that the wine, the cheese and the Streisand were designed to cheer me up. Thanks a lot for looking after me.' Next season, when Surrey played at Old Trafford, Foxy brought his mother and father to the ground. His mother, a lovely Lancashire lady, threw her arms around me and gave me a kiss. 'I've heard all about you,' she said. 'You're Percy. You're the lad who looked after our Graeme in India.'

Chapter twenty

Strange how old black and white pictures slow down the action

THERE is a picture which hangs on the wall of the Committee Room at the Oval which shows Jack Hobbs and Andy Sandham batting against Oxford University in 1926. Oxford, quite clearly, are on the attack for their captain has set a field of two slips and a gully, silly mid-off and silly mid-on. Then the eye is taken by the distant scoreboard, which proves that appearances are deceptive; the Surrey total is 428 for no wicket. The modern cricketer would look at that picture and chuckle, since the folly of setting an attacking field to that kind of total is all too obvious, but the thought of attempting to stem the flood with pragmatic field placing had plainly never crossed the captain's mind. In similar vein, I often smile at the story of the county player of bygone days who confessed that he could not combat the spin of the great Tich Freeman. 'He always does me,' said the pro, 'always gets me out caught at long-off.' The fact that he may have struck half a dozen boundaries before holing out in the deep was of no consequence. In the end, Freeman had got his man.

That attitude did not perish with the twenties, indeed, it lingered in modified form all the way through to the late sixties. I remember Colin Cowdrey remarking in 1972 that the greatest change to have overtaken cricket in his career was the fact that people had started to think about the game. The harder they thought, the greater the changes; and two factors were largely responsible for transforming the face of English cricket. In 1968, we witnessed an invasion of the cosy and traditional game by a small army of overseas players. They were not merely fine players, they were the best in the world: Barry Richards at Hampshire, Rohan Kanhai at Warwickshire, Mike Procter at Gloucestershire, Majid Jahangir at Glamorgan and a chap called Sobers at Nottinghamshire. I welcomed their arrival because I felt that the English public had the right to watch the best cricketers that contracts could buy, and I also became aware of how much these people could teach us. When you bowled to Richards or Kanhai you had to work harder and think more deeply or accept the punishment they were all too willing to provide. When you batted against the pace of Procter, you were required to analyse your technique and sharpen your reactions. The new men brought new and exacting standards and the English professionals had to meet them in order to survive. In the end, of course, the numbers of overseas players grew to unreasonable proportions and the emergence of domestic talent was stifled until the introduction of the rule which limited foreign players to one per county. But the initial impact on English cricket was stimulating and exciting and a tired old game had received the injection which it needed so badly.

The other factor which brought about change was the introduction of wide-scale one-day cricket with the John Player League in 1969. Until that time, the English professional had only one technique to learn. It was a method for playing three-day county cricket, and he acquired it, perfected it and carried it around with him like a badge of office. Now it was different; now there were bonus points, run-chases, slogging, unorthodox fields, manufactured shots and a heavy concentration upon results. People said it was a different game, and they were right. But this game demanded the kind of adaptability, discipline and physical fitness which would have crippled many of the old cricketers who were rushing to decry it.

The repercussions of these changes were enormous. Within a few years there was a levelling-off in the quality of Test sides. Whereas in the good old days a visit from India, Pakistan or New Zealand was an open invitation to English players to go for their shots and pick up a few cheap wickets, inside a decade the likes of Farouk Engineer, Javed Miandad, Imran Khan, Asif Iqbal, Glenn Turner and Richard Hadlee were emerging as players who could face us on more than equal terms. There were no more soft touches, partly because other countries were producing an increasing number of talented cricketers, but also because so many of them were receiving their cricket education in the English counties.

Beyond question, the game became more physical, outrageously so in some instances. I believe that the balance between the physical and the technical sides of cricket has been seriously disturbed by the pace and hostility of the fast bowlers from the West Indies who, on occasion, have made the game not only unwatchable but virtually unplayable. Yet such are the pressures for success that if England could produce bowlers of similar attitude and quality, we would

*Patrick's hat tricks . . .
even Test matches should have their lighter moments*

doubtless use them in the same fashion as the West Indies have done this past decade. Indeed, we might have been even more ruthless. I do not care to think, for instance, to what use Douglas Jardine or Tony Greig might have put a quartet like Holding, Marshall, Garner and Roberts. But they would have been wrong, just as the West Indies are wrong.

It was bowling of this speed and recklessness which produced the innovation most venomously scorned by the old brigade. 'In my book, a batsman with a helmet is a batsman with a white feather,' said one former Test cricketer. 'In my day, nobody would have worn it.' The truth is that in his day nobody would have needed to wear it. Certainly the likes of Ray Lindwall and Keith Miller were fast and dangerous, but the code under which they operated did not allow them to intimidate tail-enders, the players most in need of protection. Lindwall once told Jim Laker that if he had to bowl him bouncers to get him out, then he would give up the game. Such gallantry would find no place in the ruthless climate of modern cricket. In any case, Lindwall and Miller were unique in their own era, nobody else was performing with their pace and hostility. In the next match a batsman could return to the mundane task of subduing ambitious medium-pacers. In these days, when a player is confronted by pace in match after match, a form of protection is necessary and sensible. As the roads filled with cars and those cars travelled at increasing speed, we brought in seat belts and nobody, in my recollection, suggested the mass distribution of white feathers when the legislation was passed. One-day cricket made helmets more essential than ever, with its limitation of fifty-five or sixty overs and the need to score off as many balls as possible. When a ball is bowled short, it has to be hooked or avoided. The decision, against a fast bowler, is taken in one fifth of a second. If you should decide to duck and the ball is not quite short enough for that course of action, why should you be physically penalised for making the wrong, almost instant, decision? Several of the old players would have been literally frightened in such a situation, since it was no secret that some of them were unable to play fast bowling. In their day, they could get away with this deficiency by scoring their runs off the other bowlers, but in this age of blanket pace, a Test player who cannot play fast bowling is a man whose Test career will be brutally brief.

I find it heartening that the old players with the greatest insight into the problems of modern cricket are the men whose talents I held in the highest esteem. Tom Graveney, the very epitome of the English professional, enjoys the understanding of a man who once faced and handled Hall and Griffith. It would be easy for Tom to join the blimpish chorus of complaint, but he is a man of independent mind, and he knows that the game grew no more easy when he ceased to grace it. Jim Laker was another; solid, thoughtful and unspoiled by his own genius. And Kenny Barrington, who faced the first worrying wave of West Indian pace bowling, was never quick to criticise men who earned their living by making decisions in a split second.

Fred Trueman is different, since he genuinely believes that the game began to disintegrate on the day he hung up his boots. He was a great bowler, with enviable skill, control and imagination, but nothing will convince him that he was not the fiercest, most hostile performer who ever played the game. And yet, on a rain-interrupted day during the Old Trafford Test of 1984, the evidence appeared in flickering black and white film in the England dressing room. The BBC were killing time by showing the memorable 1963 series between England and the West Indies when Fred appeared on screen; tossing back his head, trundling to the wicket and sweeping into the delivery with that incomparable action. And a buzz swept round the room: 'I thought he was meant to be quick . . . no wonder they didn't need helmets . . . he's only lively medium.'

Now those players had spent most of the summer suffering the slings and arrows of Michael Holding, Joel Garner and Malcolm Marshall. They had been mercilessly abused for their failure to handle fierce and brutal pace and F.S. Trueman had led the critical pack, telling all who would listen how he would have loved to bowl at these incompetent English batsmen. Yet as they stared at that screen, every one of those batsmen would gladly have elected to face the young Trueman rather than the demons which awaited them when the rains moved away from Old Trafford. I bumped into Fred some time later. He had seen the same film and he had the grace to appear slightly embarrassed. But only slightly. 'Isn't it strange,' he said, 'how those old black and white pictures slow down the action?' There is no doubt that in his era, Fred was perceived as an intimidating bowler — partly by virtue of his ability to bowl bouncers but also because of his verbal jousting with batsmen, much of which was provocative. Fred's hostility did not however reach the unacceptable levels so often witnessed today.

There have been times, I confess, when I would cheerfully have condemned Denis Compton to the fate of facing Michael Holding on a green wicket and without a helmet. But such is the charm of the man that his impatience with modern cricket is easily forgiven. Compton is possibly the most modest sportsman I have ever met. Having spent many hours in his company, I have yet to hear him speak about himself. He will readily discuss the gifts and talents of

CHAPTER TWENTY

others, but he seems genuinely to see himself as a rather unremarkable person. I never had the privilege of playing with the vintage Compton, but one small incident in a benefit match in 1977 gave me an inkling of the incomparable performer he must have been. We were playing on a big turner at Charterhouse and it was announced that for every six that Compton hit, the benefit fund would receive £10. Since I was the beneficiary, I made quite certain that Denis was well provided with acceptable invitations. He was then in his late fifties, a plump figure in spectacles, and he had not held a bat for several years. But he played the enticing off-spin in the approved manner and chipped me easily over wide mid-on and mid-wicket. Eventually he reached his half-century and I decided that we ought to try to get him out. As my arm came over, I ran my fingers down the other side of the ball to deceive him with a leg cutter. Denis came down the wicket, picked up his bat, shaped for the conventional shot then paused and gasped. 'Oh!' he shouted ... and this heavy figure with indifferent eyesight hit the shot inside-out and lifted the ball over extra cover for four runs. I was incredibly impressed. The natural instinct of an extraordinary cricketer had spotted a wrong 'un and given it the treatment.

It was in brief moments like that I realised just how much men like Compton could offer the game, and this was a point I tried to convey to the younger players at Surrey. On one occasion, Alec Bedser came into the dressing room as Chairman of Cricket and talked about the season ahead. I warned the young players to listen carefully. We knew that Alec, like all the old ones, would constantly refer back to the way things were. We knew he was out of sympathy with many of the trends in the game and that he may not have appreciated the full impact of all the changes over the years. But he had been a great player and he was a substantial authority on the game. He should not be argued with or contradicted and certainly he should not be dismissed, because he would have pieces of rare advice and solid guidance to offer. He was a cricketing man who had made a deep mark on the game and he deserved absolute respect.

I would extend the same respect to the other major figures of former years; to Laker and Graveney, Barrington and Compton, Trevor Bailey and Godfrey Evans. All were great players and their greatness would have been apparent in any era, yet they would have been tested by the dramatic and demanding changes of the modern game. I rather doubt that Mike Gatting would allow even Fred Trueman to bowl to Hobbs and Sandham with two slips and a gully, silly mid-on and silly mid-off. And the scoreboard showing 428 for none.

*Robin Jackman —
He loved cricket as he loved life,
indeed, he rarely drew a distinction*

Chapter twenty-one

Be very certain about it, Perce.
You're a long time not playing

THERE are men who are born with a burning desire to become captain of England and there are others whose idea of heaven is to lead out a county side. As one whose leadership qualities were never glaringly obvious, I never understood those dizzy aspirations. After dipping my toe into the Surrey captaincy on several occasions over the years, I found that it detracted from my enjoyment of the game and impaired my performance as a player. In any case, captains were not always appreciated as warmly as they might have been. I remember playing down at Cardiff after Robin Hobbs had taken over as captain of Glamorgan. He had been chosen for the role late in his career, partly because of his experience but largely because of his exuberant nature, Glamorgan being a county which needed frequent applications of optimism. Hobbs batted low in the order, at ten or eleven, and he bowled infrequently, which seemed to puzzle the Welsh customers. On the day in question, the Surrey captain Roger Knight was putting in an all-round performance, picking up a few wickets and scoring stylish runs, and as I wandered the boundary one of the Glamorgan members called to me. 'Percy,' he said, 'you're very lucky with your captain. He bats and he bowls. Our one does bugger-all.' Captaincy, I decided, was a task best avoided.

I led the side for several games at the start of the 1985 season when the county captain Geoff Howarth was on Test duty with New Zealand. After an injury to Sylvester Clarke we signed Tony Gray from Trinidad and as Tony was an overseas player Geoff Howarth was unable to return to the side as we were not allowed to play both. Full time captaincy did not appeal and I thankfully passed on the job to Trevor Jesty. One of the reasons for my reluctance was the powerful influence which Micky Stewart exerted on the team as manager. I told him that captaining Surrey was like driving a car with only one hand on the wheel. His enthusiasm and his drive for perfection led to frustration and as a result Micky became far too involved in decision-making, even to the extent of over-ruling the captain on occasions. The team was becoming confused and the authority of the skipper was being undermined. Fortunately for English cricket, Micky learned a host of valuable lessons from his experience as Surrey manager and after his exhilarating success with the England team in Australia in 1987, he became the obvious, indeed the only, candidate for the permanent job of England manager.

At the start of the 1986 season, the committee at the Oval decided that the venerable Percy was just about the only candidate for the job of county captain. Things had not worked out for Trevor Jesty, nobody else was pressing a convincing case, so they handed the post to their slightly reluctant and extremely senior pro. I was still enjoying my cricket, but I had started to become nostalgic for the old days at Surrey. I regretted the passing of cricketers like Howarth and Knight, I missed the sunny, smiling Intikhab more than I could say. And most of all I missed Robin Jackman.

If anybody could find a way of bottling Jackman's energy, zest and full-hearted commitment, then the future of cricket would be safe for the next century. He believed in the game and he believed in himself. In his early years, he would take a cheap cruise to South Africa each winter and arrive at the dockside with nothing but a couple of cases and a willingness to play cricket with anybody who might be able to improve his game. He loved cricket as he loved life, indeed he rarely drew a distinction. Even the accidents which regularly afflicted him were accepted with the same relish as his triumphs. Now cricketers, as my tales of Tony Lock and Roger Tolchard may have suggested, are not invariably seen at their best in restaurants, and Jackman was no exception. On his first date with Yvonne, the lady he was to marry, he took her to an elegant restaurant and bribed his way to the best table. They were greeted by an unctuous head waiter who made great play of Jackman's cricket fame and settled them by the side of the dance floor. Trouble arrived with the soup. As it was set before him, Jackman swept open his napkin with a flourish ... and discovered, too late, that it was the cloth which contained the croutons. Small pieces of Jackman's toast covered the entire restaurant. They settled on the piano keys, they rattled on the snare drums, they lodged in the singer's hair and they crunched beneath the feet of the shuffling dancers. Even by Jackman's standards it was a spectacular disaster and the tale flew around the county circuit like

CHAPTER TWENTY-ONE

a news flash. It was Jackman who offered me a piece of serious advice when the first thoughts of retirement entered my head. 'Be very certain about it, Perce,' he said. 'You're a long time not playing.'

There was no Jackman and no Inty to help me cope with the pressures of captaincy, but I trusted that all those years of experience would see me through. Micky Stewart had become Director of Cricket and while his advice was willing and invaluable, I was given the control I had requested. There were, inevitably, problems. I greatly respected the technical ability of Geoff Arnold as a coach, but I found myself protecting players from the consequences of his insensitive man-management. I also found that the management board was attempting to play too great a role in the cricket side of the club and I knew that behind the scenes, Stewart and Alec Bedser were having to fight fiercely to maintain cricket's independence from outside interference. But the main problems were those which are common to every modern cricket captain. People who have seen close-up pictures of Mike Gatting's face in the course of a one-day match may have some small intimation of the calculations which are racing through his mind. I would walk off the field on Sunday evenings feeling mentally and physically shattered after having taken a thousand decisions during the afternoon. Pressure is at its worst when you are defending a moderate total. You have a bowler like Sylvester Clarke at your disposal; when do you bowl him? Do you try to save him until the death when the big slog is on, or do you bring him in early to push them behind the clock and hope that the additional tension will deliver wickets? You have a lot of quick fielders and one or two camels; have you got your quick men in the right positions, at long off and long on for the drivers, square of the wicket for the nickers and nudgers? If the nimble fielders are not seeing enough of the ball, at what stage do you change your field? Where do you position your fast bowlers so that they are not running from end to end of the ground between overs? Are they good enough to field in those positions? The run tally and the over tally are closing down, and the remaining overs must be shared effectively between the available bowlers. One of them may have a slight injury; do you risk him and if so for how long? And all this is going on in the knowledge that somebody has decreed that if you don't get your overs bowled within the allotted space of time, you will be fined for a slow over-rate. This causes certain problems when Ian Botham is in his most expansive mood, and the temptation is to post your best fielders outside the ground so that the ball can be returned more quickly and the subsequent fine avoided.

The burden is enormous and it is one which cricket captains of an earlier age were not required to carry. Of course, there were some

*And so I face the final curtain . . .
walking off the Oval for the last time
on a September evening in 1986*

CHAPTER TWENTY-ONE

things which were unchanging and unchangeable, as I realised when I met Geoffrey Boycott up at Headingley. Where once he had spoken only of runs and Yorkshire, now he had added the subject of money to his repertoire. He was a wealthy man, even before people started to leave him large sums in their wills, and now he had to face the problems of high finance. Should he buy a helicopter? Some people said that was a good investment. Or should he stash the stuff away in his bank and watch it grow like a white rose? On balance he tended to favour the bank. 'Hard decision, Boycs,' I said. 'But it's the sort of thing everybody has to face.' And he nodded, gravely.

I was becoming reconciled to the fact that this would be my last season in cricket. I was fit and forty, I knew that I could have gone on for a few seasons, but there was life outside cricket and it was time for me to face up to it. I knew I would need a lot of luck if I was going to be completely happy. I was involved in several commercial ventures and I wanted to explore the possibilities of attaching them to first class cricket. I would still retain an involvement with the game through my committee work with Surrey, and I realised that while I might not be burning to play the game, I should still be burning to remain a part of it.

As the day drew nearer, the prospect of leaving became more difficult to face. Strange little thoughts kept racing through my mind. After all those years, I had come to know just about everybody on the county scene; umpires, secretaries, dressing room attendants, office staff, they would all call a greeting to Percy. It seemed a pity to walk away from so many friends.

But the deed had to be done, and after leading Surrey to third place in the championship, I took my leave on a grey September evening at the Oval. We were playing Leicestershire, and I was strangely moved when Peter Willey, the most undemonstrative player in the game, wandered across to say farewell. 'Every time I've ever been to the Oval, you've been here to bowl at me,' he said. 'I'll miss you, Perce.' I remember blinking at him. 'If he's going to miss me,' I thought, 'then I must have made my mark.'

Farewells at Surrey were always profoundly emotional occasions. I have seen strong, worldly Test cricketers break down in tears as they stood in the Committee Room and attempted to convey their feelings about the county and the game. And I had cried with them as I watched my friends depart; Stewart, Jackman, Intikhab and others whose careers and fine company I had shared. I asked Diane to be there to support me, and I clutched a glass of orange juice throughout my reception, fearing that the very taste of alcohol would unhinge my feelings. But, by sheer chance, I was saved. For the first time they decided to hold the ceremony in the Long Room with all the members present, and the size of the crowd thankfully diluted the tension of the moment. The first person I had seen undergo that farewell ceremony at the Oval was Bernie Constable. Suddenly the years had flashed past and it was my turn. I spoke of all the men whose faces were passing before me at that moment; of Lock and Barrington, of Arnold, Storey and Long; of Jackman, Roope, Thomas and Butcher, all the way through to Martin Bicknell, the seventeen-year-old colt who stood and watched wide-eyed, just as I had watched those many years before. It was difficult, but I managed to complete the speech and say the things I wanted to say.

A few hours later, I left the ground with Micky Stewart. 'Am I glad that's over,' I said. 'And I'm so pleased we held it in the Long Room. If we'd been in the Committee Room, with just a few people there and all that emotion pressing in, I know I'd have broken down.' And Stewart smiled, the tight, faintly sadistic smile of the English professional cricketer. 'No,' he said, 'it wasn't nearly so emotional, was it? We'll have to change that arrangement next year.'

Although he was smiling, I knew he meant every word; tears were traditional on such occasions, and tradition must be respected. And as Stewart spoke, I fancy I heard a grunt of approval rumbling down from the dark, empty Surrey dressing room. Sandy Tait was reaching across a quarter of a century to put me in my place.

CAREER STATISTICS

BATTING

Comp.	M	I	NO	Runs	HS	Avge	50
Test	25	37	4	206	33	6.24	—
FC	554	585	156	4,867	75*	11.34	3
Int.	1	1	0	4	4	4.0	—
NW	34	20	7	77	14	5.92	—
BH	71	32	16	124	19	7.75	—
JPL	209	104	38	492	22	7.45	—

BOWLING

Comp.	Overs	Mdns	Runs	Wkts	Avge	BB	5wkts	RpO	Cts
Test	1,108.2	279	2,976	67	44.41	6.79	3	2.68	15
FC	16,760.5	4,821	42,648	1,607	26.53	9.57	60	2.54	186
Int.	10	1	20	0	—	—	—	2.0	—
NW	353.4	77	961	37	25.97	3.34	—	2.71	6
BH	691.4	127	2,168	76	28.52	4.11	—	3.13	11
JPL	1,413	130	5,795	213	27.20	4.27	—	4.10	41

List of Illustrations

	Page
Pat Pocock — *Peter Basden, M.P.A.*	7
Micky Stewart — *Adrian Murrell, All-Sport*	11
Sandy Tait and Pat Pocock — *Central Press Photos Ltd.*	15
Jim Laker and Tony Lock — *Sport and General Press Agency*	21
Ken Barrington — *Patrick Eagar*	25
Pat Pocock — *Adrian Murrell, All-Sport*	29
Alan Knott — *Adrian Murrell, All-Sport*	33
John Edrich — *Adrian Murrell, All-Sport*	41
St. Vincent, West Indies — *Adrian Murrell, All-Sport*	45
Port of Spain, West Indies — *Adrian Murrell, All-Sport*	45
John Snow and Tom Graveney — *Patrick Eagar*	49
Basil d'Oliveira — *Patrick Eagar*	57
Syd Buller — *Press Association*	65
Geoff Boycott — *Patrick Eagar*	69
Micky Stewart — *Patrick Eagar*	73
Pat Pocock and World Record Trophy — *South London Newspapers*	77
Bishen Bedi — *Press Association*	81
Kandy, Sri Lanka — *Michael King, All-Sport*	85
Karachi, Pakistan — *Adrian Murrell, All-Sport*	85
Tony Greig — *Adrian Murrell, All-Sport*	89
Gary Sobers — *All-Sport*	93
H.M. The Queen and Pat Pocock — *Daily Mail*	101
Brian Close — *All-Sport*	109
Malcolm Marshall and Pat Pocock — *Patrick Eagar*	112
Michael Holding and Pat Pocock — *Patrick Eagar*	112
Intikhab and Pat Pocock — *Waddell*	119
Ian Botham — *Adrian Murrell, All-Sport*	127
Alec Bedser — *Adrian Murrell, All-Sport*	129
David Gower — *Adrian Murrell, All-Sport*	131
Eden Gardens, Calcutta, India — *Adrian Murrell, All-Sport*	135
David Gower — *Adrian Murrell, All-Sport*	139
Mike Gatting — *Adrian Murrell, All-Sport*	143
Graeme Fowler — *Adrian Murrell, All-Sport*	147
Pat Pocock and family — *Peter Shelley, Daily Express*	151
Phil and Frances Edmonds — *Patrick Eagar*	151
Pat Pocock — *Adrian Murrell, All-Sport and Graham Morris*	155
Robin Jackman — *Patrick Eagar*	159
Pat Pocock — *private*	163

Index

Ahmed, Saeed 60.
Ahmed, Younis 71, 72.
Alam, Intikhab 60, 62, 70, 72, 118, 119, 161, 162, 164.
Ali, Abid 82.
Alley, Bill 111.
Allott, Paul 125.
Ames, Les 40.
Amiss, Dennis 32, 83, 92, 95, 100.
Arlott, John 97, 133.
Arnold, Geoff 32, 71, 72, 82, 94, 162, 165.
Azharuddin 149.

Bailey, Trevor 107, 158.
Ballesteros, Manuel 125.
Ballesteros, Severiano 125.
Barber, Bob 54.
Bari, Wasim 61.
Barlow, Eddie 88.
Barrington, Ken 14, 16, 19, 24-27, 36, 39, 43, 51, 53, 58, 123, 126, 157, 158, 165.
Bedi, Bishen 80, 81, 82, 83.
Bedser, Alec 71, 128, 129, 158, 162.
Benaud, Richie 123.
Bethell, Arthur 46.
Bicknell, Martin 165.
Birkenshaw, Jackie 79.
Botham, Ian 42, 99, 124-127, 130, 134, 140, 142, 162.
Botten, Jackie 67.
Boyce, Keith 91, 94.
Boycott, Geoffrey 23, 24, 36, 38, 43, 51, 52, 55, 66, 67, 69, 72, 92, 95, 96, 118, 164.
Brearley, Mike 31, 35, 123, 126.
Broad, Chris 125.
Brown, David 32, 36.
Brown, Tony 134, 136, 137, 150.
Budd, Lloyd 111.
Buller, Sydney 64-66.
Burge, Peter 23.
Burki, Javed 100.
Burton, Richard 83.
Buss, Mike 74.
Buss, Tony 74.
Butcher, Alan 165.
Butcher, Basil 42, 43.

Camacho, Steve 42.
Cardus, Neville 58.
Carey, Mike 144.
Carr, Donald 80, 86, 92.
Cartwright, Tom 56.
Chandrasekhar, B. S. 82, 83.
Chappell, Ian 54, 88.
Clarke, Sylvester 120, 160, 162.
Close, Brian 24, 27, 97, 108, 109, 110, 111, 114, 126.
Coleman, Bernie 115.

Compton, Denis 99, 157, 158.
Constable, Bernard 19, 165.
Cook, Nick 123.
Cook, Sam 28, 50.
Cope, Geoff 117, 118.
Cottam, Bob 79, 106.
Cowans, Norman 142.
Cowdrey, Chris 141, 142, 144.
Cowdrey, Colin 36, 37, 39, 40, 43, 44, 47, 48, 51, 52, 53, 54, 61, 126, 153.
Cowdrey, Penny 44.

Daniel, Wayne 108, 110.
Denness, Mike 82, 90, 91, 92, 94.
Dev, Kapil 145, 146.
Dexter, Ted 24, 58, 125.
d'Oliveira, Basil 36, 40, 42, 54-57, 61.

Edmonds, Frances 146, 148, 151.
Edmonds, Phil 106, 142, 146, 148, 149, 151.
Edrich, John 14, 23, 36, 38, 39, 41, 70, 71, 75, 110, 113, 120, 123.
Ellison, Richard 125.
Emburey, John 122, 149.
Engineer, Farouk 154.
Evans, Godfrey 52, 158.

Flavell, Jack 28.
Fletcher, Keith 24, 32, 79, 82, 86, 87.
Forbes, Carlton 26.
Foster, Neil 145.
Fowler, Graeme 125, 130, 144, 145, 146, 147, 150, 152.
Fredericks, Roy 91, 92, 96.
Freeman, Tich 153.
French, Bruce 144, 150.

Gandhi, Indira 133, 136.
Garner, Joel 130, 156, 157.
Gatting, Mike 141-145, 158, 162.
Gavaskar, Sunil 145, 149.
Gibbs, Lance 42, 43, 52, 53, 94.
Gifford, Norman 79, 136, 150.
Gilliat, Richard 70.
Gleeson, John 55.
Gower, David 123, 124, 126, 131, 133, 136, 138, 139, 140, 141, 142, 144, 145, 146, 148, 150.
Graveney, Tom 36, 38, 39, 40, 43, 47, 49, 51, 53, 58, 59, 123.
Gray, Tony 160. 126, 156, 158.
Greenidge, Geoffrey 74.
Greenidge, Gordon 64, 70, 110.
Greig, Tony 82, 86, 87-92, 94-96, 108, 115, 116, 123, 156.
Griffith, Charlie 39, 42, 43, 47, 51, 156.
Griffith, Mike 74.

Hadlee, Richard 154.
Halfyard, Dave 98.
Hall, Wes 39, 42, 43, 47, 113, 156.
Hampshire, John 27.
Harman, Roger 23.
Harper, Roger 130.
Hayes, Frank 94, 95, 108.
Hendrick, Mike 95, 108.
Higgs, Ken 39, 54.
Hobbs, Jack 153, 158.
Hobbs, Robin 50, 160.
Holder, Vanburn 108.
Holding, Michael 97, 107, 108, 110, 111, 112, 113, 114, 124, 130, 156, 157.
Holford, David 42, 43.
Howarth, Geoff 160, 161.
Hutton, Len 16, 17.

Illingworth, Ray 27, 55, 63, 67, 68, 117.
Ilyas, Mohammad 60.
Iqbal, Asif 154.

167

Jackman, Robin 72, 74, 98, 118, 121, 124, 159, 161, 162.
Jackman, Yvonne 161.   164, 165.
Jackson, Les 122.
Jahangir, Majid 60, 153.
Jameson, John 104, 105.
Jardine, Douglas 90, 156.
Jepson, Arthur 64.
Jesty, Trevor 160, 161.
Jones, Jeff 36, 53.
Joshi, Dulip 74.
Julien, Bernard 87, 91, 94, 108.

Kallicharran, Alvin 87, 88, 90, 91, 92, 96.
Kanhai, Rohan 42, 91, 99, 153, 154.
Keeping, John 18.
Khan, Imran 154.
Knight, Roger 120, 160, 161.
Knott, Alan 32, 33, 34, 36, 52, 53, 79, 95.

Laker, Jim 14, 18, 19, 20, 21, 44, 47, 71, 156, 157, 158.
Laker, Peter 86.
Lance, Tiger 88.
Lander, Chris 144.
Lamb, Allan 124, 134, 137, 148.
Lashley, Peter 43.
Lawry, Bill 54.
Lewis, Roy 74.
Lewis, Tony 64, 79, 80, 82, 83, 84, 123, 134.
Lillee, Dennis 95.
Lindwall, Ray 156.
Lloyd, Clive 42, 47, 48, 53, 91, 92, 94, 97, 111.
Lloyd, David 146.
Loader, Peter 71.
Lock, Tony 14, 19, 20, 21, 36, 48, 50, 51, 52, 53, 54, 71, 90,
Long, Arnold 70, 71, 74, 165.   161, 165.

Mack, Andy 121.
Marks, Anna 144.
Marks, Vic 144.
Marlar, Robin 79.
Marshall, Malcolm 112, 130, 141, 156, 157.
Marshall, Roy 70.
May, Peter 134.
McIntyre, Arthur 19, 27, 74, 118.
Merton CC 18.
Merton C of E Secondary Modern 18.
Miandad, Javed 154.
Milburn, Colin 39, 40, 61, 104.
Miller, Keith 99, 156.
Modi, Rusi 84.
Mohammad, Hanif 60.
Mohammad, Mushtaq 60, 106.
Mohammad, Sadiq 128.
Moore, Ian 16.
Morley, Jerry 74.
Murray, Deryck 42, 53, 91, 99, 110, 113.
Murray, John 59.

Nawaz, Sarfraz 60.
Newton, Derek 120.
Norris, Angela 136.
Norris, Percy 136.
Nurse, Seymour 42, 43.

Old, Chris 86, 94.

Packer, Kerry 103, 115, 116.
Parkar, Ramnath 82.
Parker, Jack 50.
Parks, Jim 36, 43, 74.
Peel, R. 130.

Pepper, Cec 64, 71.
Pocock, Diane 20, 22, 30, 35, 46, 56, 78, 84, 86, 136, 149,
Pocock, Toby 149, 151.   151, 164.
Pocock, Sami 78, 86, 149, 151.
Pollock, Graeme 88.
Pollock, Peter 88.
Popplewell, Nigel 126.
Prideaux, Roger 55, 60, 61, 74.
Procter, Mike 20, 67, 153, 154.

Redpath, Ian 54.
Rhodes, Wilfred 142.
Richards, Barry 64, 70, 126, 153, 154.
Richards, Vivian 108, 110, 121, 126.
Ridding, Bill 111.
Roberts, Andy 94, 97, 108, 110, 113, 156.
Robins, Derrick 103-106.
Roope, Graham 71, 72, 165.
Rowe, Lawrence 91, 94.

Sandham, Andy 153, 158.
Selvey, Mike 108.
Shackleton, Derek 122.
Smith, Mike 106.
Smith, Peter 144.
Snow, John 36, 37, 38, 47, 49, 52, 53, 54.
Sobers, Gary 42, 43, 51, 52, 82, 90, 91, 92, 93, 96, 97-102,
Spencer, John 74.   108, 126, 154.
Spencer, Tom 100, 101.
Srikkanth, Krishna 139.
Steele, David 108, 113.
Stewart, Micky 14, 16, 19, 24, 27, 28, 50, 55, 70-75, 80, 120,
Stewart, Sheila 50, 71.   161, 162, 164, 165.
Storey, Stewart 16, 72, 75, 165.
Streisand, Barbra 150, 152.
Surridge, Stuart 26, 71.

Tait, Sandy 13-17, 165.
Tate, Fred 142.
Tate, Maurice 142.
Taylor, Brian 64.
Thomas, David 120, 165.
Thomas, Bernard 136.
Thomson, Jeff 95.
Tindall, Ron 16, 26, 27.
Titmus, Fred 36, 37, 42, 44, 54, 67, 118, 120, 148.
Tolchard, Roger 105, 161.
Trueman, Fred 27, 126, 157, 158.
Tucker, Bill 16.
Turner, David 70.
Turner, Glenn 154.
Tyson, Frank 107.

Underwood, Derek 32, 55, 61, 62, 68, 79, 86, 117.

Vorster, John 56.
Vengsarkar 149.

Walcott, Clyde 47.
Walters, Doug 54.
Willett, Barry 18.
Willey, Peter 164.
Willis, Bob 72, 94.
Wilson, Don 68.
Wimbledon Technical College 18.
Wood, Barry 108, 110.
Woodcock, John 144.
Wooller, Wilf 90.

Yardley, Jim 72.

168